masters of
the swindle

TRUE STORIES OF CON MEN, CHEATERS & SCAM ARTISTS

WHITE STAR PUBLISHERS

WS White Star Publishers® is a registered trademark
property of White Star s.r.l.

© 2016 White Star s.r.l.
Piazzale Luigi Cadorna 6
20123 Milano, Italy
www.whitestar.it

Project editor and editorial assistant: ICEIGEO, Milano
(Gianni Morelli, Paola Paudice, Chiara Schiavano, Carlo Batà)
Translation: Jonathan West, Canice Murray
Editing: Max Rankenburg

ISBN 978-88-544-1063-3
1 2 3 4 5 6 20 19 18 17 16

Printed in Malta

Text by: Claudio Agostoni, Carlo Batà, Giulia Gatti, Enzo Gentile,
Margherita Giacosa, Lorenzo Marsili, Silvio Mignano, Gianni Morelli,
Roberto Mottadelli, Giorgio Oldrini, Paolo Paci, Paola Paudice,
Chiara Schiavano, Alfredo Somoza

masters of the swindle

the swindle

TRUE STORIES OF CON MEN, CHEATERS & SCAM ARTISTS

Edited by
Gianni Morelli and Chiara Schiavano

Contents

Introduction

I make people believe something is real
when they know perfectly well it isn't.

John Lithgow (actor)

- If I must be honest . . .
- Nooo, why? You can tell a lie . . .
Who'll notice?

Giuliana De Sio and Massimo Troisi
in the movie *Ricomincio da tre*

With the invention of truth, it was inevitable that false-
hood would follow. And since then, one has always
needed the other, by definition. Although they have both assumed thousands of identities, it is the lie, especially, that has
always enjoyed the theater and disguises: usually unexpected,
lies are sometimes tragic, often amusing. But the most spec-
tacular of his maneuvers is certainly deceit. And if we at this
point bring gullibility into play, the die js cast. From Eve's
Apple, to the Trojan Horse, to our times, deceit and credulity
have never gone on vacation. It is by their union that we have
the swindle.

In this volume we have collected recent stories, from the
late nineteenth century to the present. To do this we have
selected forty tales of raconteurs, jugglers, artists of illusion,

gamblers, and scientists of imaginative finance. We present here people who have worked with words as much as with time, with the gaps in the fabric of reason, with the most impossible possibilities, and with the most contradictory evidence, making of these phenomena objects, figures, and events that are more real than reality.

Many of these projects, especially the financial ones, were meticulously constructed around vulnerable and vague points on the border dividing legality and illegality. Many others are simply mental masterpieces. Seldom in these cases can we resist the temptation to take the side of the "evil genius," to cheer for a *finale* that crowns the show.

So here we speak of artists and their works, although what we narrate is only the tip of the iceberg, because what we finally know about the crime is only a small part of the "business" that was discovered.

Many books have been published on swindles and great swindlers; so in collecting these stories, we have placed emphasis on genius, on the idea behind a con, on the theatrical. We have especially considered the value of "historical" cases, but have also included funny cases, and cases with extraordinary style, both in clothes and in methods.

For this reason, this collection lacks less noble or theatrical examples. It lacks medical and food scams, or structural scams – the exploitation of vulnerabilities in the global economy by multinationals to evade taxes, or economic liberalism without rules, for example. It also lacks the world of virtual finance, the so-called derivatives market; it lacks the sophisticated and extremely costly devices designed by technicians and engineers to escape controls and to beat the competition, and so on.

A Sucker's Born Every Minute

If we had to describe three qualities indispensable to the swindler, these would be super *sangfroid*, extreme creativity, and delusions of omnipotence, not necessarily in that order. Take, for example, the Cacicco MacGregor who sold the rights to the lands of the Principality (fictitious) of Poyais in Central America almost two centuries ago (*The Paper Empire*); or Victor Lustig who, after selling the Eiffel Tower, went on to con no less than Al Capone (*Count Victor Lustig*); or Han van Meegeren, who copied Vermeer so well as to be discovered only when he himself spontaneously confessed (*The Vermeer of Deventer*) – because, in the end, if no one else knows, what's the fun?

Often the basic ingredient of the swindle is a false identity. Around the false identity, the swindler then constructs a castle of cards which, contrary to every prediction, becomes more stable than anything made of stone and concrete. This stability owes a lot to coincidence, but it is also due to the swindler's vigorous ability to improvise. The example par excellence was Frank W. Abagnale, forger, and then fake pilot, fake pediatrician, and fake lawyer, and in the end true anti-scam consultant for the banks and the FBI (*A Hundred Thousand Times Frank*). But there was also Friedrich Wilhelm Voigt, in Prussia of the middle of the nineteenth century, who played a handsome trick on the little town of Köpenick (*The Captain of Köpenick*); and also, more recently, the young Spanish rascal who was present at the coronation of the King of Spain and who, without any kind of fame or fortune, got himself on popular TV talk shows (*El Pequeño Nicolás*).

Speaking of titles, the sale of more or less noble titles has always aroused the desires of the vainest, and is inevitably one of the richest veins for the swindler, from those near the top, with the British crown (*A Despicable Life*), to those on the streets of Cuba in the middle of *Revolucion* (*One Christmas, at Habana Hilton*).

Sometimes, on the other hand, it is a case of Columbus' egg (a brilliant idea that seems obvious in retrospect): stealing the *Mona Lisa* in order to push up the prices of copies already in circulation (*Stealing the Mona Lisa*). Or, in another scam, a man, respected in his field, put on exhibit archeological discoveries which were, needless to say, forged: he changed the parameters of human history (*The Piltdown Man*). Or, by retro-dating fossils and artifacts by hundreds of thousands of years, a researcher undermined a country's past and identity (*The Hand of God*). And why let Earth be the domain of what's possible? The sky is no limit for those who want to believe in other worlds, in new horizons for the Universe (*Alien Autopsy*).

Among the favorite scenarios, obviously banks stand out. More often than not, swindlers shoot high, going after massive and practically impenetrable institutions, like the Bank of England at the end of the nineteenth century (*The Cashier's Fault*) or, just a few years ago, the Vatican's bank (*The Mystery of the 24-hours Billionaire*). The most important financial circuits in the world are also inevitably targets (*The Hyena of Wall Street*). But in modern times, capital runs along telephone lines (*A Ten-Million Dollar Phone Call*) and also, once the suckers on the web have taken the bait, money travels in the more traditional way in the form of cash in sealed envelopes (*The Republic of Eden*).

And then, here they are, the indefinable artists who became examples for posterity. Take Ferguson (or Furguson), for example, who probably never even existed (*The Swindler's Swindle*); or Ponzi, about whom hundreds of thousands of pages have been written in biographies, studies, and articles, all providing various and diverse data and theories (*Carlo Pietro Giovanni Guglielmo Tebaldo Ponzi*). In the end, in one way or another, his name recurs in this book several times.

That Thin Gray Line

These are the masters of deceit: their stories are often incredible, and sometimes extraordinary novels in four dimensions.

On novels, a warning: to study these personalities often means entering a world in which the researcher's efforts at objectivity are often sorely tested. The facts (names, addresses, dates, events, methods), even as they appear in official documents from interrogations and police reports, are in many cases difficult, if not impossible, to confirm. And indirect confirmation (witnesses, journalists, biographers, relatives) is simply unreliable. In most cases, the main sources of the information we have are those directly involved: the swindler and his victim. However, one of the unwritten rules of swindling is never to tell the truth about oneself. Add to this principle, which basically stops in its tracks the search for even an approximation of the truth, the numerous motives the other actors in this comedy have for keeping quiet. So what the researcher turns up are verbose justifications of credulity, and statements by those who, for different reasons, want to inflate their accomplishments. They are all writers, basically, the con men and their victims alike.

Builders of truth and reality, like us, they just want to set the record straight.

Thus, in the most "studied" stories, there are numerous additions of dubious authenticity: imaginary reconstructions, urban legends, myths, colorful descriptions that may come off as completely arbitrary, nicknames, abstruse words pronounced and written as if to make history, the superimposition of different figures and events, one over the other, and so on. To be brief, to give them a suitable name yet again: there are little deceits throughout. In some cases, there is more than one addition, more than one little deceit. Some are obvious. Some are well hidden.

There are certainly some in the stories we tell here, as indelible as the color of time. In fact, the contrary would be surprising. It would be surprising if when we spoke, or wrote, of swindles, everything were really in its place, that we were in the presence of Incontrovertible Truth. It would be surprising and perhaps a little sad.

The swindle and deceit are hidden everywhere, particularly where we do not expect them: in articles of the largest newspapers, in most television shows, in the supermarket, in the condominium meeting, in the office, on the tram, in your home, in this book, perhaps in these very lines.

Great swindlers ignore the line between lies and the truth because it's negligible, indefinite, fleeting, changeable. But also because they know, on that line, sooner or later, we all slip.

Gianni Morelli

The Paper Empire

Gregor MacGregor (United Kingdom)

He sailed from Scotland to the Americas, to fight with the liberta-
dores. He was a man of arms. But he was also a genius, capable of
inventing a country from nothing. A charming fellow, he convinced
seasoned bankers in England to believe in an imaginary country
and to exchange their pounds sterling for a currency that didn't
even exist.

Caracas, 1811. At twenty-five, Gregor MacGregor was made
a colonel in Francisco de Miranda's liberation army. Later,
on Margarita Island, Simón Bolívar would make him a general.
He liked the sun in Venezuela, admired the flight of the *guaca-
mayas*, the great red, blue, and yellow parrots that always flew in
pairs, scratching the tropical sky with open wings and long and
narrow tails. And he liked the shivers at Josefa Andrea Aristeguieta Lovera's touch, the heat of her skin, her Venezuelan beauty,
the brilliance of obsidian in her eyes. Many years later, it was
strange to recall – in that long history of fraud and lies – that

there was a time when General MacGregor fought seriously. He participated in the conquest of Cartagena. He saved the Venezuelan army in an extraordinary retreat, protected by thousands of Arawak archers. Bolívar commissioned him to raise a liberation army on the island of Hispaniola, in the Antilles.

In Honduras

One day, he received three gentlemen who were introduced as delegates of the Río de La Plata and patriots of Argentina and of *El Cono Sur* (the southern half of South America). They were worried about their brothers in Eastern Florida, a territory still under Spanish control even fifty years after the American Revolution – an injustice, they said, that needed to be corrected.

MacGregor agreed to help. With his army, he drove the Spanish out of Saint Fernandina, on the east coast of Florida. But, contrary to what the three gentlemen had promised, the people there were not ready to stand against the Spanish and fight for the green cross on a white ground, the flag that Mac-Gregor waved for the new free land.

He felt betrayed. He had to abandon Florida and return to Venezuela, where soon after he found himself in the inglorious debacle of Porto Bello, in Panama, 1819. His escape from the battlefield became the supreme test of his ability to transform the truth with words: in his account, the retreat was a heroic defense against superior Spanish forces.

So he ended up in Honduras, under King George Frederic Augustus of the Miskito people. Augustus ceded the territory of Poyais to him. It was from the king that MacGregor first heard about the pseudo territory, a region not recognized by authorities

---

A Poyais dollar, the bill printed in Scotland by the Bank of Poyais.

On December 24th, 1786, Gregor McGregor was born in Edinburgh, Scotland.

In 1803, he enlisted in the British Navy.

In 1805, he married Marie Bowater, who died a short time later.

In 1811, he arrived in Venezuela, after being made a colonel. He fought in the Latin American wars of independence against the Spanish crown with Sucre, Diego de Miranda and Simón Bolívar.

In 1817, he assaulted Saint Fernandina, on Amelia Island, a Spanish stronghold in Florida.

In 1819, Bolívar's Great Colombia was establishead.

In 1820, he returned to London with his second wife, Josefa Andrea Aristeguieta Lovera, a Venezuelan Creole. A short time later, he announced that King George Frederic Augustus I had granted him the territories of the Principality of Poyais, facing the Gulf of Honduras.

In 1821, with Major William J. Richardson, he opened offices of the Legation of Poyais in Edinburgh, Glasgow, and London.

In September of 1822, the first ship of colonists bound for Poyais left London. The travelers had changed their pounds for Poyais dollars.

In October of 1822, MacGregor issued 2000 Poyais government bonds for a total of 200,000 pounds.

In January of 1823, a second ship left for Poyais. When the colonists arrived, they found those who had preceded them in September severely tried by tropical fevers and other hardships. Poyais did not exist, nor did its cities, nor its immense agricultural and mining wealth, nor the peaceful natives. There was nothing in Poyais, apart from rain forest and mangroves. Of the 240 colonists who left England, 47 survivors returned to London after one year in the wilderness. Another five ships bound for Poyais were intercepted and turned back.

In London, Poyais became a scandal. Many still defended MacGregor, who was in France at the time, organizing French colonists for Honduras. Meanwhile, he transformed Poyais into a Republic with a completely new constitution.

In August of 1825, in London – where in spite of everything Poyais continued to attract colonists – MacGregor received another loan against bonds of the Republic for 300,000 pounds.

In France, the swindle organized by a marine company in league with MacGregor emerged. There was a trial in April, 1826. MacGregor and his accomplices (except for one man, who escaped to Belgium) were mysteriously acquitted and released. MacGregor returned to London, where he was arrested and detained for one week. He then announced that he had been elected *cacique*, or leader, of the aborigines in the Republic of Poyais.

From 1828 to 1837, he issued bonds for 800,000 pounds and sold land, but it was becoming more and more difficult to attract interest in Poyais. Complicating matters was also the fact that the new king of the Miskito in British Honduras, Robert Charles Frederic, was selling the same land to lumber traders. And to top it off, a mysterious company called Upton, with no connection to MacGregor's operation, had opened a Poyais office in London. 1839. MacGregor moved to Caracas, and asked for a War of Independence pension. He died there in December, 1845.

---

overseas. The exact dimensions of Poyais, and the language and traditions of the place, these were issues open to debate. But Mac-Gregor took the story a step further: he invented a country to sell to Europeans. He envisioned an autonomous state, with its own currency, the Poyais dollar, with a tricameral parliament, and an army, and ambassadors. Even more incredible: he would have representatives of King George Frederic Augustus present at the coronation of Britain's new king, George IV, at Westminster.

London, 1821

From his great office on the Thames, they watched the intense activity of the construction of a new bridge in London. His wife, Josefa Andrea, smiled at him. Gregor laughed openly: "My love, they believe . . . Can you believe it? They believe us." It was too good to be true. He had invented a country that did not exist: a crescent-shaped stretch of the coast of Central America, the land of the Miskito, in Honduras.

He made the state. He coined the currency, designed the maps, wrote about its cities and villages, described its numerous ministers – because, as you know, in these American statelets, they have offices for everything. But at the same time, the place needed people to do the work and to make others work. "And here I am with you," he would say to potential investors, in his London reception rooms or at his beautiful estate in Essex: "There is gold, copper, silver, immense fruit plantations, sugarcane, and grazing land. If you are without fear you have a future there."

They wanted to hear more of the battles, of the bullets that hissed by, centimeters from his head, of the orders shouted on the quarterdeck of the flagship in the middle of a Caribbean hurricane. In the uniform of a senior officer and commander of a troop of Miskito, he makes a big impression on the women of London, while the bare shapely shoulders of Josefa Andrea mag-

TO THE ACTION, THE COLONIZATION ENTERPRISE

From the report of the foreign minister to the Parliament of New Grenada. Bogota, 1857: "Two recent actions of the British Government deserve attention. Two treaties stipulated with the Republic of Honduras, one of which regards the restitution of a stretch of coast from the Gracias a Dios River to San Román, more than 150 nautical miles attributed to what is known as the Mosquito Kingdom, where the colonization enterprise of General Gregor MacGregor, with the title of Cacicco of the Poyais, took place in recent years."

netize the eyes of the men. The princely couple quickly scale the social ladder of high society.

Inebriated by the music of the orchestra and the scent of brandy, MacGregor half-closes his eyes, satisfied.

Legation of the Principality of Poyais, 1822

The doorbell was ringing behind the mahogany front door. There always seemed to be a crowd wanting to come inside. In his London office, the high windows of leaded glass filtered out the noise of the frenetic to and fro of the city. Horses and carriages, porters' carts, a newsboy on the corner announcing that the Liberation Army had cleared the Spanish from another stretch of the Andes. MacGregor smiled: he knew the men with the pompous titles very well. Marshall Antonio José Francisco de Sucre y Alcalá, General Brigadier Simón José Antonio de La Santísima Trinidad de Bolívar Ponte y Palacios Blanco: they were sweeping the Spanish crown from half the continent. It was because of them that an American fever was spreading throughout European stock exchanges.

"I'm a genius," MacGregor told himself, looking up at the framed charter on the wall: Prince of Poyais by the grace of God and the King of the Miskito, George Frederic Augustus I. Next to the charter was a map of the immense territory skirting the bay of Honduras.

Beyond the bronze-studded mahogany doors of his office, a line of English men had formed. All of them came to buy government bonds issued by the state. His State.

"And here they come," MacGregor thought, preparing his notes, his presentation on the Poyais economy, the investment

WHO WAS GREGOR MACGREGOR?

MacGregor was not a simple con man. He was a standard-bearer for Zelig, a Pirandello-esque character. In Europe he was known above all for the "Poyais Scheme": he invented a state, created a complex but false structure, printed currency, sold titles of state on the stock market that were guaranteed by imaginary natural resources. In Venezuela, on the other hand, he still figures in accounts of the liberation wars. He was an independence hero, even though a minor character; a smaller Garibaldi, buried with full honors in a Caracas cathedral. But he was also the generous victim of bogus rebellions which he himself supported with blood, sweat, and tears, as happened when false emissaries from Río de la Plata entangled him in an attempt to liberate Eastern Florida.

opportunities, the diplomatic assignments and the titles of nobility that accompanied, in some cases, the purchase of a generous amount of titles of state. "If you believe in the crown of the Miskito, the Cacicco of Poyais will compensate you," he said, receiving his underwriters with open arms.

In the Cathedral, with the Fathers of the Republic

Caracas, 1839. Beyond the window, in the garden, the large mango was laden with unripe fruit. "What was I thinking," MacGregor said, searching for a ripe one. "Maybe I didn't fully believe that anyone in the end would actually embark for the Principality of Poyais, and discover the deceit."

He had escaped to France, been arrested, tried, and miraculously acquitted. He had returned to England, been arrested again, and acquitted once more. And incredibly, after all that, thousands of investors continued to believe and subscribe in his titles of state. What had been going for 300,000 pounds he raised, with a magical touch, to 800,000 pounds, every penny guaranteed by his rank of Cacicco di Poyais.

After Josefa Andrea died, he returned to Caracas, to where it all began. Bolívar was dead too. An era had come to an end. The new president, José Antonio Páez had granted him a war pension.

Although he wanted to rest in peace, in the shadow of the mango, he still hoped, still waited for the colonists to come with the ships, for the Principality of Poyais to become a real thing. "Perhaps, perhaps all things considered it will not be under the mango that I will find peace," he thought. "A cathedral awaits me."

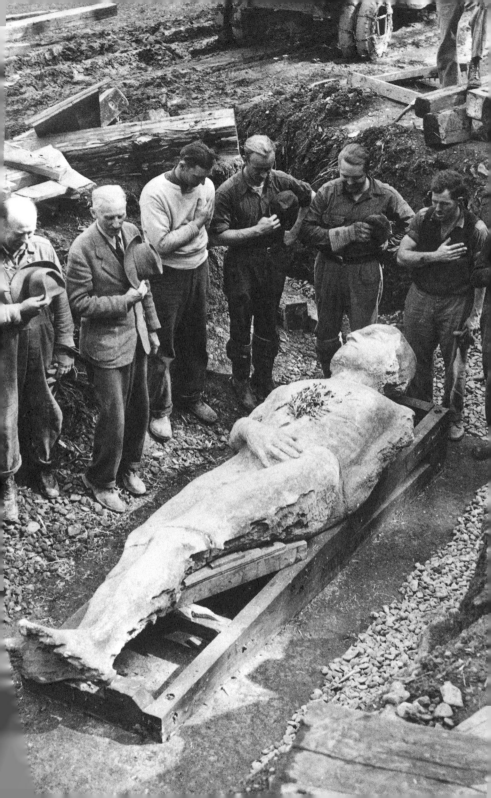

The Cardiff Giant

George Hull (United States)

When a cigar maker from New York orchestrated the discovery of a stone giant, he earned himself a tidy sum of money. The event also aroused a passionate debate among archeologists and paleontologists. The scientists disagreed on the true nature of what would soon become an attraction for curious people from all around, people willing to pay and stand in line for hours, waiting to see the phenomenon up close.

October 6th, 1869. Two men given the task of digging a well on the farm of one William Newell, in Cardiff, New York, unearthed what seemed to be a stone giant. In the semblance of a man, the object was over ten feet tall. But how did it get there, and how long had it been buried in the earth?

The idea came to the local cigar maker, George Hull, Newell's cousin, after passing through Iowa and listening to a preacher. The preacher maintained that passages in the Bible were always to be read literally. Even when what was written was hard to believe:

> *There were giants in the earth in those days; and also after that, when the sons of God came in unto the daughters of men, and they bare children to them, the same became mighty men which were of old, men of renown.* (Genesis 6:4)

Hull, who was an atheist, was skeptical about this preacher's message, and that very night, staring at the ceiling, he found a way to make fun of people's credulity, and also to scrape together a bit of money. He had just given up on his cigar company,

---

The moment of the discovery of the Cardiff Giant, today exhibited in the Farmer's Museum, Cooperstown, New York.

near Binghamton, New York, because it was weighed down with debt, and was heading out West in search of fortune, perhaps as a gold prospector. Fate, and the minister's sermon, determined that he wouldn't move too far from home before finding an unexpected source of earnings.

The "Birth" of the Giant

Hull went to Fort Dodge, a nearby town, and ordered a block of gypsum, more than ten feet long and weighing more than five tons. He said that it was for a statue of Abraham Lincoln (assassinated three years before, immediately after the Civil War) which would be erected to his memory in New York. Then he packed it all up and with some difficulty (he had to leave a piece behind to reduce the weight), sent it to Chicago, where a German sculptor, Edward Burghardt, sculpted the block into a nude prone man with his right arm on his abdomen and legs slightly crossed; the face, which resembled Hull's, bore an enigmatic smile, as if the statue itself were mocking its viewer. To make the statue seem very old, Burghardt used acid and stains; the surface was scoured with sand and sulphuric acid; the "skin" was perforated with knitting needles to create pores; the gypsum was spontaneously covered with streaks in the likeness of veins. In November, 1868, Hull transported the giant on a goods wagon to his cousin's farm in Cardiff, just south of Syracuse, where he buried the block of gypsum behind the barn. In total, he paid 2600 dollars to make and transport the statue; he promised part of his future profit to the sculptor and to his cousin. Then he returned home, waiting for the right moment to complete his plan: he knew that time had to pass before people forgot his movements and the movements of that bulky load. So about a year later, he told his cousin to go ahead and have the well dug: in no time, what emerged from the earth seemed to be a petrified giant.

The Swindle and its Fruits

Once out of the swampy ground, the Cardiff Giant quickly and compellingly became popular. News of the discovery spread rapidly. Men left work, and women brought the children: everyone wanted to go out to the farm. Newell built an awning over the giant, fenced off the area, and even hired a barker; he charged a quarter to anyone who wanted to see it. Then, because of its popularity, he doubled the price two days later. 2500 people came out to see the Cardiff Giant in one week. And soon enough the discovery became the subject of arguments all over the country. Some scholars immediately cast doubt on the authenticity of the colossus, and spoke of swindle and fraud; preachers and the faithful were of a different mind. There were those who maintained that it was a petrified man who had lived many centuries before, and those, including recognized scientists, who maintained that it was a statue sculpted by a Jesuit missionary in the previous century to awe the Native Americans. Some even stated that it was the most important archeological discovery of the century. Besides the curious, and Hull, who of course came to the farm in secret, some businessmen turned up, scenting a good opportunity; Newell, in league with his cousin, sold the giant to a consortium of five men led by David Hannum, in exchange for 30,000 dollars. The giant was then taken to Syracuse.

The Chickens Come Home to Roost

P. T. Barnum, the famous circus impresario, showed great interest and put forward 50,000 dollars to rent the giant for three months: when his offer was refused, he certainly did not give up on this chance for easy money, and had a copy made. He exhibited his copy in New York, passing it off as the original and claiming that the Cardiff Giant (not his giant) was, in fact, a fake. Hannum thus decided to sue Barnum for slander: the judge ruled that before hearing the case the authenticity of the real giant had to be proved.

In Syracuse, many skeptics went to see the fantastical giant. The opinion of Othiel C. Marsh, a paleontologist at Yale University, was brief and to the point, and left no room for doubt. The Cardiff Giant was a maladroit fake. The marks of scalpels used to sculpt it were still fully visible, as were some cracks untouched by the application of sulphuric acid. A mining engineer argued that the signs of deterioration should have been more pronounced, given the damp ground, close to a marsh, in which the giant had been found.

In Cardiff, some people remembered seeing Hull, a few months before, transporting a large, canvas-covered load; and in November of the previous year, in Fort Dodge, someone remembered hearing about Hull and large shipment he made. Some reporters also discovered that shortly after selling the Cardiff giant, Newell transferred an enormous sum of money to his cousin's bank account.

George Hull's Confession

On December 10th, Hull, cornered and fearing that his scheme was about to be exposed, moved preemptively and told the press that the Cardiff Giant was a hoax. The case between Hannum and Barnum was dismissed, because the judge ruled that it was not a crime to describe a fake giant . . . as a fake. And in 1870, Mark Twain, in *A Ghost Story*, had the ghost of the Cardiff Giant appear in a Manhattan hotel room, imploring to be buried again. The giant ends up so confused that he begins harassing the copy of himself that Barnum had made.

Hull went back to making cigars. He did try his luck, a few years later, with another fantastical giant, this one about nine feet tall, and with a tail. He buried it in Colorado. The scheme was immediately revealed, and he lost a lot of money. He died a few years later, alone and forgotten.

BARNUM, APART FROM THE (FAKE) CARDIFF GIANT . . .

P. T. Barnum had all sorts of sideshow attractions. There was Joice Heth, a blind woman, almost entirely paralyzed, presented as the wet nurse of George Washington (which would make her more than 160 years old); there was the Feejee Mermaid, a creature with a monkey's head and a fish's tail; there was General Tom Thumb, a dwarf who imitated famous people, including Napoleon, and who at five years old drank wine and at seven smoked cigars. (Thumb was also the protagonist of a very successful tour in Europe, during which he met Queen Victoria and Tsar Nicholas I). The Siamese twins, Chang and Eng Bunker, who were born in Siam and from whom the syndrome takes its name, were the fathers of ten and eleven children, respectively. And there was Anna Swan: weighing eighteen pounds when she was born, Swan grew to nearly eight feet tall, and incredibly managed to marry a man who was taller than she was.

A Diamond Mine

Philip Arnold and John Slack
(United States)

In 1848, the California Gold Rush filled the valleys and streams of the West with unscrupulous men, men sure or hopeful that in the subsoil lay immense fortunes waiting to be found. One day, decades later, two prospectors from Kentucky walked into a bank with a deerskin bag . . .

It was a February morning like any other. Two men entered the Bank of California in San Francisco: one of them had a rifle in his hand, the other had a deerskin bag. They were an unsavory duo, so much so that the cashier was afraid they were outlaws. However, they only asked to deposit what the bag contained into the bank vault: even if they did not reveal what it was, they let the cashier peek furtively inside. It held nothing less than diamonds, rubies, and sapphires.

The News Spread Rapidly

These two unusual clients were Philip Arnold and John Slack. As a young man, Arnold had worked in an artisanal workshop, taken part in the war against Mexico and, a few years later, in 1849, he had arrived in California. Over the next twenty years, he worked in a mine, accumulating enough money to buy a farm in Kentucky (where he was born), raise a family, and put away a nice nest egg. By 1870, he had a position as assistant accountant in the Diamond Drill Co., a company that produced drills with diamond bits. Around his fortieth birthday, he told his cousin, Slack, a taciturn and apathetic man, about his plans.

The night before that February morning, they paid a visit to George Roberts, an extremely ambitious and unscrupulous businessman who was well known for his love of risk. When Roberts saw these two dust-covered men come into his office, and listened to their account of how they'd found dozens of rough diamonds in a remote corner of the Indian territories, the businessman promised to keep their secret until the extent of the diamond mine they claimed to have discovered could be ascertained. According to the two men, sapphires, emeralds, rubies, and other precious stones could be found in the mine near the surface. After they left, in fact, Roberts immediately contacted the manager of the Bank of California, William C. Ralston, which was exactly what Arnold and Slack were hoping he'd do.

The geologist Clarence King, seated in the center, and his team of expert workers, who are carrying out an inspection in the mine.

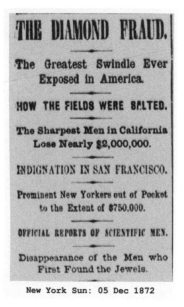

A New York Sun *article.*

Before long, all of San Francisco knew about those diamonds. The city had ballooned after the completion of the transcontinental railroad in 1869, and currently numbered about 150,000 inhabitants; it was the fulcrum of the West Coast economy.

Ralston and Roberts thought they were dealing with two country yokels, but Arnold and Slack were in reality consummate actors who were making fun of them: there was no mine, and they had not found those precious stones.

The Swindle Yielded More than the Most Optimistic Expectations

After depositing the treasure, Arnold and Slack disappeared. They returned to the city several months later, this time with a sack brimming with precious stones. The scheme, already consolidated, was then repeated around the country.

Before investing large amounts of capital in their enterprise, however, Ralston and Roberts called an expert mining engineer, Henry Janin, and asked him to verify the authenticity of the stones. Janin travelled with Arnold and Slack out to Western Wyoming. Getting off the train, Arnold and Slack blindfolded the engineer until, after a four-day horse ride, they reached the mine – close to what is today called Diamond Peak, in northwest Colorado. There, clearly visible on the ground, were gemstones of every kind. It was June 4th, 1872. After almost a year and a half, it was the decisive moment. Janin's response was positive, and so, on his return to the city, other businessmen quickly expressed interest in the mine: among them were Nathan Rothschild and Charles Tiffany, two men who certainly knew something about gemstones. It was precisely a trusted employee of Tiffany, in New York, where a sample had been brought to him, who dispelled every doubt, valuing the stones at 150,000 dollars, when they were barely worth a few thousand. The employee was an expert in cut, polished stones; he'd never been asked to value rough stones. But in order to hide his inexperience, he examined each of the stones carefully, and then exclaimed:

Gentlemen. These are without any doubt precious stones of enormous value!

It was a stroke of luck for Arnold and Slack, who eventually sold the stones for 650,000 dollars. But to the investors, that was a derisory sum, considering what the mine was probably worth.

Mine? What Mine Would that Be?

The geologist Clarence King, a guru in his field who knew the Rocky Mountains inside out, did not believe the story in the least (from the few data in his possession, among which Janin's account). He succeeded in reaching the mine and began to dig: he found one or two stones just under the ground, but deeper down there was only earth. He concluded that stones had been brought in from elsewhere, given that – as geologists, experienced miners, and mining engineers know – different types of stones are never found in the same deposit. King went to the nearest telegraph office and told Ralston about his discovery. The news was given large headlines on the front pages of all the newspapers. It was November, 1872, and *The New York Times*, which had been skeptical from the outset, was finally able to write sarcastically, in a December 6th article, that the most incredible aspect of the affair was that:

> *Businessmen and capitalists noted for their shrewdness have been deceived, like those of San Francisco.*

The Tiffany staff appeared, in spite of his high-sounding name, to be completely unreliable. The swindle itself would also seem a little simple and crude, if one did not consider the uncontrolled euphoria, verging on hysteria, aroused by the so-called gold rush.

Ralston refunded 80,000 dollars to the twenty-five investors swindled, but could not recover the money given to Arnold and Slack. In 1875, after the failure of his bank, his body was found floating in the water of the San Francisco Bay. King effectively became a national hero, recognized by public opinion as a principled man of science who triumphed over the greed of the swindlers. In 1879, he was appointed the first director of the prestigious United States Geological Survey.

Rise and Fall of two Gold Prospectors

But how did Arnold and Slack devise what the *San Francisco Chronicle* at the time described as the "the most enormous and brazen swindle of our times"? Since they had not become rich by finding diamonds, why not at least try to make people believe that they had? The idea, which was both simple and flawless, had been to purchase, first in Arizona, and then even in London and Amsterdam, rejected diamonds, remains of cut stones from South Africa, and to then scatter them across the presumed mine. The initial investment, which in any case was large, was 35,000. Then all they had to do was to play the part of two run-of-the-mill gold prospectors.

Once he had pocketed the money, Arnold returned home to Elizabethtown, Kentucky, reinventing himself as a successful entrepreneur and banker. Of course, the people he'd defrauded sued him, but these cases were settled without too much trouble. He died some years later from the after-effects of pneumonia, which he contracted after being wounded in a duel with a rival banker. Slack, on the other hand, disappeared from public life after squandering his fortune. He opened a casket shop in St. Louis, and then found work as a grave digger in White Oaks, New Mexico. Then, around the time he turned eighty, he himself ended up in the ground.

THE GOLD RUSH DID NOT STOP

The news of the discovery of such a rich deposit unleashed a brief and intense psychosis which drew thousands of prospectors once more into the American West. Mining exploration companies sprang up like mushrooms, and businessmen all over the country bought stock in them. Even Tiffany and Rothschild had a part in the mania . . . To have an idea of the climate of those years, in April, 1870 – a few months before the appearance of Arnold and Slack – an article in the *Tucson Weekly Arizonian* read: "We have found it! The greatest treasure ever discovered in the continent and without a doubt the greatest that the human eye has ever seen." The treasure was a silver mine which gave rise to a small town nearby. Still, as someone later commented: "That much-praised, epoch-making quantity of silver wasn't enough to even make a buckle." Such cases, reported one after another, were usually identified as swindles. Arnold and Slack's plan, in this regard, insofar as it made them rich while making fun of the financial elite of the time, was a terrific success.

The Cashier's Fault

Austin Biron Bidwell, George Macdonnell,
George Bidwell and Edwin Noyes
(United Kingdom)

There were four in the gang that robbed the Bank of England in 1873, getting away with an undisclosed – but considerable – sum. They were exposed by a banal error, and were eventually identified by the Pinkerton National Detective Agency, due to the intervention of which the forgers will be captured.

Two distinguished gentleman entered Edward Hamilton Green's elegant tailors in London one day early in 1872. They were leaving on a trip to Ireland and needed adequate apparel at short notice. One of the two was introduced as a rich magnate of the American railways: his name was Frederick Albert Warren. While the tailors took their measurements, they heard Warren speak to his friend of his worries. He feared that during the trip they might be robbed of the cash they were carrying. It was too much for such a journey. Then he asked the shop owner if he had a safe, and if they could leave the money in his safekeeping while they were away, Mr. Green answered that it was indeed too much money to keep in a tailor's safe. But at his bank, he went on to say, they would certainly be able to open an account in his name. As soon as they finished selecting the cloth, all three headed for the Burlington Gardens branch of the Bank of England, a short distance from the tailor's shop. There assistant manager Robert Fenwick was happy to open an account for a rich American introduced by such a reliable customer as Mr. Green, the tailor. Signatures were signed, checks issued, handshakes exchanged and everything was done and dusted.

At least Twenty Aliases

But who were the two gentleman who entered Mr. Green's shop that afternoon? Mr. Warren was in reality one Austin Biron Bidwell, counterfeiter, thief, and swindler who, although only twenty-seven years old, already had to his credit a long résumé of crimes for which he had used at least twenty false names. The other, who signed himself on that occasion as Edward R. Swift, was George Macdonnell. Born to a wealthy family, he attended Harvard medical school, but came to be known as a refined and cultured forger who was heard to remark:

Swindling is an art – wretched and despicable, but art.

There were four in the gang. Also in London that day was George Bidwell, Austin's older brother. A slightly debauched womanizer, George wasn't entirely trusted by the others. Next there was Edwin Noyes Hill, who played the part of Mr. Warren's secretary; he looked after more modest, day-to-day logistics. In the preceding years the four had traveled Europe far and wide, from Berlin to Marseilles, from Dresden to Bordeaux to Lyons,

---

Etching from 1873 showing a moment from the trial, at the Old Bailey in London, of Austin Biron Bidwell, George Macdonnell, George Bidwell, and Edwin Noyes.

sowing fake bank titles everywhere they went. They had accumulated a substantial amount of money. They usually returned to the United States or Latin America in the winter, waiting for the Old World to forget about them.

A Telegram

It was Macdonnell who noticed, by chance, that the checking procedures performed by the celebrated Bank of England – fondly called the "Old Lady of Threadneedle Street," a reference to the location of its headquarters – were slow but superficial. The procedure, in fact, was vulnerable to anyone who could work carefully and quickly. He sent a telegram to Austin Bidwell, convening the entire gang in London. They rented an apartment at Piccadilly Circus and planned their attack against the most important credit institution in Europe. The method was simple. Using the account opened at Burlington Gardens, the four organized a whirlwind round of purchasing and selling exchange notes, presenting these at discounts to various credit institutions. Often they asked for cash, or even gold in exchange for the bank transfers. Then they immediately bought United States bonds. When the Bank of England finally got around to checking Mr. Warren's credit, the money he and his gang had already stolen was long gone. In a few weeks, the swindle assumed enormous proportions, which the Bank of England never exactly quantified. Estimates put the loss between a quarter and half a million pounds sterling.

William Pinkerton Arrives

The Pinkerton National Detective Agency, in the person of William Pinkerton (one of the founder's two sons) was already on the case. Following a tip, he'd gone to London, where he had been informed that something was about to happen. One day, walking along the Strand with Inspector John Shore of Scotland Yard, he recognized two men from identity photos he had memorized. He told Shore that they had just passed the two most dangerous American counterfeiters and swindlers, Macdonnell and Bidwell. He said, with uncanny premonition,

Those two could easily rob even the Bank of England.

However, Pinkerton was outside his jurisdiction and had no authority to intervene; moreover, Macdonnell and Bidwell hadn't committed a crime in England, or rather none that either Shore or Pinkerton were aware of. They were therefore limited to simply watching the two suspects. The detective enumerated some of their legendary enterprises in the United States, including their collaboration with corrupt police officers in New York.

A Grain of Sand

Suddenly the mechanism jammed. Everything had been running so smoothly. But then the gears ground, a speck of sand caught in the mesh. Perhaps through haste, Hill had taken a number of Rothschild exchange bills to pay into a bank, and forgotten to put the date of issue on two of these. He left the bank promising to return the following day to withdraw the money. The conscientious cashier who handled the transaction decided to do the distracted customer a favor, so to save time concluding the payment the following day, he called Rothschild to find the missing dates. But, to his great surprise, the issuing bank knew nothing of either titles or customer. It was clear that the bill of exchange was false. The cashier told his manager about the swindle. When Hill arrived to withdraw the money the following morning, Scotland Yard was waiting for him. Inspector Shore, recalling his chat with Pinkerton, put two and two together, and the manhunt began.

Guards and Thieves, Escapes and Pursuits

No sooner had Macdonnell realized that something was amiss, than he left Piccadilly without paying the rent. The landlady was furious, checked the apartment to see if there was anything left behind and found only traces on a blotting pad where the im-

AH, THE DAMNED MOTHER-IN-LAW

Austin Bidwell had courted the young and beautiful Jeannie Devereux for a long time. She was eighteen, came from a modest family, and her meddlesome mother dreamed of a respectable marriage for her. When her daughter accepted the attentions of this eccentric young man (who was often absent for reasons unknown) she tried everything to end the relationship. But Jeannie Bidwell was fascinated by Bidwell. He bought her expensive gifts and promised a wealthy future for them both. They were all set to marry – they were in the car on the way to the church, in fact – when the prospective mother-in-law exploded in fury, sending everything up in the air. So they tied the knot in Paris, far from that vexing woman, and on the eve of the great swindle of the Bank of England. When Hill was arrested, Bidwell and his bride sailed for Cuba, combining his escape with their honeymoon. The mother-in-law discovered that the newlyweds were in the Caribbean when she received a letter from Jeannie, who had written to give her the news. The woman identified where they were from the stamp and put the pieces of the jigsaw together: she'd heard of the bank robbery in England, and she lost no time in reporting them to Pinkerton. William, having verified that Bidwell was indeed in Havana, went down to the island to arrest him. And that's what he did. Bidwell, for his part, bribed his guards and escaped for a time; but he was quickly caught, and sent to London for trial.

postor had dried a letter. One word remained legible: Thulluginon The woman called the police and Inspector Shore immediately discovered that a ship by that name was leaving Le Havre for New York. The French police arrived at the port too late. The ship had sailed. Macdonnell was on board. The police on the other side were notified; the fugitive would be caught at the docks. Still, Macdonnell had an escape: Captain Jimmy Irving, of the New York Police, was an old acquaintance, even an accomplice. But corrupt officers can be greedy. So when the fugitive made the mistake of lying about the amount of money he had with him – declaring 83,000 dollars and not 125,000, comprising a part to be delivered to Macdonnell's sister– the captain didn't blink, and the fate of the swindler was sealed. They sent him back to London.

George Bidwell escaped with his usual retinue of women, but was caught in Edinburgh. His brother, Austin, was caught in Havana by Pinkerton.

A Pistol-Packing Judge

All four were tried at the Old Bailey in London in August of 1873, a few months after the heist. The security measures were extraordinary: the delinquents had many sympathizers in England, and the bank, many enemies. Demonstrations or attacks on the court were feared. Perhaps because of these fears the verdict was determined in record speed: in fifteen minutes, all four, the Bidwell brothers, Macdonnell, and Hill were found guilty. They were sentenced to life in prison. Although they didn't serve to the bitter end, Bidwell and his gang did spend a long time in prison. George spent the years writing a weighty book (of 560 pages) on how he had brought the Old Lady of Threadneedle Street to the brink of crisis.

CASSIE L. CHADWICK.
1904.

A Hypnotic Gaze

Elizabeth Bigley (United States)

One afternoon in the spring of 1902, the open carriage hailed by James Dillon, a lawyer, pulled up in front of a luxurious residence on the Upper East Side, at the corner of East 91st and Fifth Avenue. The man watched astonished as the woman riding with him stepped down from the carriage, walked straight up to the front door, and rang the bell. It wasn't the sort of thing you saw every day, considering the man inside the place – the woman's "daddy" – was the multimillionaire steel magnate, Andrew Carnegie.

Some people, right from birth, identify with the name they are given and the family they are born to. Others like to switch, endlessly, from one identity to the next.

From her teenage years, Elizabeth Bigley decided she'd be of the second category. At thirteen, in Norwich, Ontario, she went down to the local bank and presented a letter claiming that her uncle had left her a substantial sum of money as a legacy. The letter, written by Elizabeth herself, was so convincing that the teenager obtained a loan from the bank. Several months went by before the deception was discovered, at which time young Elizabeth was arrested. But she was only ordered never to do it again, and then released. From that moment on, her career as a con artist took off.

The Legacy on Visiting Cards

At twenty-two, she repeated and perfected her adolescent scam: she gave her benefactor a face, and a name, a London address, and a profession. This time, the legacy amounted to 15,000 dollars. She even printed visiting cards with the words "I am an heiress

---

Curly hair, cocksure attitude, elegant clothes: one of the most famous images of Elizabeth Bigley.

to 15,000 dollar" and began to show them to gain respect and credibility with storekeepers. From time to time, she would enter a store, choose an item of a lower price than the value on her bank checks, and take the change in cash. Thus she left with something she wanted, and a pocket full of money.

She later moved to Cleveland, in the United States, to stay with her sister Alice, who had recently married. Alice welcomed Elizabeth with open arms, and Elizabeth promised to stay just long enough to find a job and a place to live. Alice did not know that it was not sisterly love that had prompted Elizabeth's visit. But soon she found out. Her husband wised her up to what was happening when he discovered that Elizabeth was using their furniture as a guarantee to obtain loans from the banks. Furious, Alice and her husband kicked her out, and from that moment Elizabeth Bigley vanished and Madame Lydia DeVere was born.

With a Crystal Ball

In 1882, in the guise of the respectable widow Lydia DeVere, Elizabeth stole the heart (and wallet) of a wealthy doctor, Wallace S. Springsteen. The doctor was enchanted by Lydia's hypnotic gaze, but also by the opportunity, floated by her, of getting his hands on a "little" castle in Ireland, which Lydia was due to inherit. Springsteen decided to make her his wife. But the marriage didn't last very long (eleven days), for as soon as the photos of the wedding were published in *The Plain Dealer*, Springsteen's home was besieged by Lydia's creditors. Once more, she was shown the door.

The woman did not give up. Masquerading as a fortuneteller, Mademoiselle Marie Rosa, Elizabeth spent four years in and out of several marriages and prophesizing, at the end of which she was arrested yet again for financial fraud.

But not even prison could stifle her ambition. After three years in prison, Elizabeth was released and, in the guise of Cassie L. Hoover, opened a brothel. It was around that time that the hardened con artist met her future husband, the rich widower Leroy Chadwick, a man who would play a fundamental role in her career: thanks to him, in fact, she would succeed in pulling off her greatest scam, in which she passed herself off as the illegitimate daughter and heiress of the famous Andrew Carnegie.

An Open Secret

In 1897 Cassie officially became Cassie Chadwick, the name with which she would go down in history. Her marriage to Chadwick let her plunge into a world of luxury and claim a place in high society, even though, as she soon discovered, her husband wasn't as rich as she thought. However, she knew how to exploit situations. Among her husband's acquaintances was James Dillon, an attorney friend, who was known as being a bit of gossip.

In the spring of 1902, Cassie took a train from Cleveland to New York. Once there, she made for the Holland House Hotel, where "by chance" she bumped into none other than James Dillon. After briefly chatting with the man, feigning surprise at meeting him like that, she politely asked if he wouldn't mind escort her over to her father's place. Dillon agreed and was flabbergasted when Cassie had him stop the carriage right in front of Carnegie's home.

Cassie had calculated everything. She knew that in order not to arouse suspicion she had to stay in the Carnegie mansion for about a half hour. While Dillon, in his car, imagined a loving conversation between Cassie and her father, inside the house Cassie killed time talking with Carnegie's housekeeper, inquiring about a woman named Hilda Schmidt, a maid, Cassie said, who had once worked for the millionaire and had asked her for a job.

Half an hour later, Cassie returned outside and got back into the car. As she was doing so, she accidentally dropped a promissory note (previously forged), which Dillon picked up. His jaw dropped: the note was for 2 million dollars, and there was the signature of Andrew Carnegie.

Cassie thus revealed her "secret": she was nothing less than the steel magnate's illegitimate daughter. Oppressed by a sense of guilt, Carnegie continued to give her, in secret, huge sums of money in the form of promissory notes. The multimillionaire had also

THE SCROOGE MCDUCK OF STEEL

But who was Andrew Carnegie? The perfect embodiment of the American Dream, the multimillionaire king of steel had emigrated from Scotland with his parents, of humble origin, in search of fortune. In 1865, he founded his company, the Carnegie Steel Company, in Pittsburgh, and in a few decades it constituted a business empire. This made him the second richest man in the world, after John D. Rockefeller. At sixty-five, Carnegie sold his company to a banker to dedicate himself entirely to philanthropy: his passion for culture inspired him to found more than 2500 libraries, to donate 5 million dollars to the New York Public Library, and to finance museums and research centers bearing his name around the world. Carl Barks is said to have also been inspired by him when he created his famous character, Scrooge McDuck. Old Uncle Scrooge was, in fact, a Scot of humble origin who had emigrated to the United States and become one of the richest people (or rather, ducks) on the planet. We can almost hear Carnegie in McDuck's philosophy:

The world is full of opportunities for a duck who can think a little more and jump quicker than the others! And I'm accumulating experience! This young country is a good example! A place where a poor boy from Glasgow can become the owner of the richest hill in the world! They should build a monument here somewhere! A statue that welcomes people who arrive here, following their dream of becoming someone!

named her his heiress. Dillon promised not to tell anyone about the revelation. But he was a hopeless gossip, so in a matter of hours word got around town. The rest was easy. Waltzing into the Wade Park Bank the next morning, Cassie took out her first loan as the Carnegie heiress.

It Was Enough to Ask

Cassie Chadwick took out loans totaling 20 million dollars from banks like the Lincoln National Bank of New York, and the Citizen's National Bank of Oberlin (which would end up bankrupt because of this). No one dared ask Carnegie whether Cassie was actually his daughter through fear of embarrassing him. Everyone trusted that the debts would be settled with the million-dollar inheritance.

In 1904, however, Herbert Newton, a Boston banker, who demanded the immediate payment of a debt, exposed Cassie's lieu. He was made suspicious by her hesitation, and asked Andrew Carnegie to confirm the relationship. The latter denied knowing the woman. Cassie was arrested, tried, sentenced to ten years in prison, and fined 70,000 dollars.

Carnegie was personally present at Cassie's trial: he was curious to know the woman, who with so much aplomb had managed to pass herself off as his daughter and get away with it. When he was shown the famous promissory note used in the swindle, he said, referring to spelling mistakes it contained:

If anybody had seen this paper and then really believed that I had drawn it up and signed it, I could hardly have been flattered. Why, I have not signed a note in the last 30 years. The whole scandal could have been avoided if anyone had bothered to ask me.

The Burglar
Who Lived Twice

Clarence Adams (United States)

Clarence Adams was a rich librarian from Vermont. Bored with life, but with a passion for thrillers and the occult, he transformed himself into an ingenious burglar. For a long time, he was uncatchable. Then, once captured, according to one of the versions of this strange story, he invented the most far-fetched escape. It involved a sensational trick.

In 1886, the novels of Robert Louis Stevenson began to enjoy a certain popularity, also in the village of Chester, in deepest Vermont. But none of the almost two thousand inhabitants adored them as much as Chester's eccentric librarian, Clarence Adams, a man always immersed in thrillers and adventure stories, hypnosis manuals and spiritualism treatises. Though he belonged to one of the most renowned families in Windsor County, and had inherited a very profitable farm, Adams found Sir Arthur Conan Doyle much more interesting than the mud under his boots, and preferred the dark pages of Edgar Allan Poe to the ripening grain.

If any of his neighbors had shared his passion for literature, Adams would certainly have found it more difficult to carry out his plan. Or perhaps he would never have needed to: he would have banished boredom by talking of magic, Oriental philosophies, and mysterious crimes, never needing to take up such a strange pastime.

Strange Burglaries in Chester

The routine in Chester changed – slowly, as one would expect in a provincial village – in the last fifteen years of the nineteenth century. At first, people only noticed a few minor thefts, incidents that appeared to be more like jokes and tricks than real crimes. Then increasingly larger burglaries – in houses, shops and workshops – began to take place. Each time the police arrested a tramp, a drunkard, a known criminal, but guilt was promptly disproved by the occurrence of a new burglary. On the crime scene and in the local bar, Clarence Adams listened to everyone's opinions and entertained the townspeople, shopkeepers and even some policemen with his extremely personal reconstructions of the events: storybook crimes with spirits, ghosts and *feuilleton* criminals, tales so bizarre that nobody took them seriously.

A close-up of Clarence Adams.

If he had not been rich – and if he had not become a member of the Legislative Assembly of Vermont – he would have been relegated to the role of eccentric village intellectual, a slightly less noble role, but nonetheless necessary in the country scene.

In the meantime, the burglaries continued. The favorite target was the miller, Charles H. Waterman, one of the wealthiest and least educated men in the village. Sacks of grain, clothes, and stationery disappeared from the mill and its store. There were no traces of the burglar. It was not even easy to reconstruct how he broke into the buildings: it was discovered, only after some time, that the burglar unscrewed the locks of doors and windows and then screwed them back perfectly when he went out. This brilliant maneuver allowed Adams to conjecture that there were supernatural forces at work.

In July of 1902, Waterman, exasperated by investigations that never went anywhere, decided to take the law into his own hands: he placed a rifle in front of the window through which he suspected the burglar would come, and tied the trigger to the shutter. Since he was a good-hearted man, he aimed the rifle at the base of the window. Killing was not his idea of justice.

When Waterman arrived at work on the morning of July 28th, he was greeted by an unscrewed hinge. There was also a large patch of blood on the floor. They quickly founded the injured man. To their surprise, the whole of Chester discovered that Clarence Adams had just been treated for a serious gunshot wound in the leg. Nobody believed his explanation, which consisted of an unprovoked attack by two unnamed robbers. He survived the wound but could not avoid arrest.

During the trial, Adams confessed everything, explaining that he had stolen simply for pleasure. He wanted to make fun of the police and the people of Chester, who had laughed at him for his fantasies, by showing them the plausibility of the plots of his favorite books. He said nothing about possible accomplices, which the prosecution considered very likely.

The judge sentenced Adams to ten years in prison. Obviously the judge had no sense of humor, nor was he a man of letters. The officers at the state prison in Windsor were no different. So when the new prisoner asked if he could restore the run-down prison library, there were no objections. No one had ever thought of seriously dealing with those dusty shelves, and very few of the inmates wanted to use the library. Only one of the prisoners was happy about the move. He was an unusually educated man with a privileged position: thanks to his medical studies, he had become the alter ego of Dr. John Brewster, the prison doctor, to the point of standing in for Brewster in his daily duties. He became good friends with the new prisoner, the burglar who would restore the prison's library.

An Unexpected Death

According to official accounts, Adams died on February 26, 1904, after two years in prison. The cause of death was a sudden lung disease. In accordance with the wishes of the deceased, expressed in a will made a few days before, the body was entrusted not to his relatives but to a friend, a certain William Dunn, who mysteriously arrived immediately after Adams' death. It was Dunn who dealt with the burial in a provisional crypt in Cavendish cemetery. Only after the spring thaw would it be possible to bury the casket. A couple of months later, rumors began to circulate in Chester that Adams had staged his demise.

Some acquaintances maintained that they had seen him in Nova Scotia, Canada, in perfect health except for a limp caused by the gunshot wound in the leg. The merchant John Greenwood even reported speaking to him. Soon it was widely assumed that Adams staged his own death, the only way to escape from prison without having the police on his heels.

Indeed, Clarence Adams' last days in prison leave room for many conjectures. His death was so rapid and unexpected that it caught the prison doctor by surprise. Twelve hours before, he had examined the prisoner and found nothing more worrying than the common cold. There was also his will, composed in prison just prior to his death, as though Adams knew the fate that awaited him. Lastly, there was the sudden appearance of Dunn: he came for the body even before the prison governor had sent for him. Dunn's explanation? He said that Clarence had written him a few days before, telling him that he was afraid he didn't have long to live.

A HASTY EXHUMATION

When the press got interested in the case, Clarence's relations decided to have the body exhumed to end the gossip. The casket was not empty, as some had expected. But by then the body was unrecognizable. Although the remains were more or less comparable with the characteristics of Adams' body, it was impossible to establish its identity with certainty. Strange to say, the authorities took care not to verify the only detail that could shed light on the question, namely the condition of the bones of the left leg, the one hit by the rifle shot which stopped the burglaries. The investigations were quickly concluded. People saw in this the machinations of the Adams family, who wanted to end, once and for all, the scandal staining the family name. Or maybe it was to keep Clarence's second life a secret.

From Canada to Mexico. Perhaps . . .

The unofficial version of what happened next is that provided by Edward H. Smith in his 1929 book of investigative journalism, *You Can Escape*. Decades later some of Adams' fellow prisoners confirmed Smith's account to another writer, Alexander Klein, author of *The Grand Deception*, published in 1955. According to Smith, Adams planned his escape right from his first days in prison. He began by studying the habits of Dr. Brewster, and then bribed the prisoner assisting the doctor with 3000 dollars: although he remained in prison, by helping Adams, the doctor's assistant became a rich man. In the meantime, Adams also kept in touch with some of his accomplices on the outside, among whom was the so-called William Dunn. But his trump card was the exceptional prompt he found in the library: Robert Louis Stevenson, who in *The Master of Ballantrae* has one of his characters stage an adventurous death. The long, monotonous solitude of prison gave Clarence time to practice meditation and self-hypnosis.

By February, he was able to go into a trance and to reduce his heartbeat to a minimum. He pretended to be ill, made his will, and a few days later staged his death at three in the afternoon. He knew that at that time Brewster would not go to the prison to confirm the death, but would simply sign the death certificate brought to him by his assistant. And that's exactly what happened. The assistant prepared the body, explaining to the prison governor that he wanted to do it as a sign of respect for his deceased friend. A few hours later, William Dunn turned up at the prison office and took the body away before the arrival of Dr. Brewster, who was to carry out the last formalities.

Adams had thought of everything. He knew very well that in February it was not possible to dig a grave, and that being placed in a provisional crypt would make it easy to escape at night. Leaving nothing to chance, Adams asked his accomplice to obtain the corpse of a man approximately his height from the dissecting room of nearby Dartmouth College. Once he had placed the body in the casket, Adams would pay his debt to Dunn and board a train bound for Canada. According to some accounts, after being recognized by old acquaintances, he took refuge in Mexico.

We probably will never know how Clarence Adams' earthly life ended. And yet, more in this case than in any other, to ascertain the truth would serve little purpose. Because for Clarence Adams, who broke into mills and stores just for the joy of it, real life was the one lived in novels. In one way or another, the gentleman thief from Chester, Vermont, managed to turn his life into an exciting story, a tale to tell with a touch of noir, a tale little different from those living on the shelves of his library.

HYPNOSIS AND CATALEPSY

Catalepsy is a passive state characterized by slow respiratory and cardiac activity, and rigidity of posture: a person may remain in rigid positions that are also extremely uncomfortable. The first scientific studies on catalepsy were conducted in the nineteenth century by, among others, the great French neurologist Jean-Martin Charcot (1825-93) who, in the final fifteen years of his life, systematically studied hypnosis. In Clarence Adams' time, many scientific and parascientific articles circulated on the subject, as did articles on suggestion and self-suggestion techniques. The theme of apparent death was often present in the newspapers, which told phantasmagorical stories of people buried alive by mistake. It is possible that this genre of literature, besides fascinating Adams, contributed among his contemporaries to the credible hypothesis that he had staged his own death.

They Called Me Yellow Kid

Joseph Weil (United States)

Joseph Weil was born in a poor quarter of Chicago near the end of the 1800s, just like the Yellow Kid, the boy with jug ears in the historic comic strip Hogan's Alley. But unlike the child who always wore a hand-me-down yellow nightshirt, Weil, as an adult, was considered one of the most well-dressed men in the city. His made-to-measure clothes were the result not of his parents' work in their small grocery store, but of his own vivid imagination and his profound understanding of human nature, both of which enabled him to become one of the most famous (and long-lived) con-men of the twentieth century, known as the "Yellow Kid."

Brought up in a family of honest toilers, Joseph Weil soon decided that a life of hard work and sacrifice was not for him. He saw in his future success and money, so he left school at seventeen and began working as a loan-shark debt collector. Weil, young and eagle-eyed, soon learned how to turn the human weaknesses he observed in his colleagues to his own advantage; when he discovered theft and corruption spreading among his associates, instead of denouncing them to the bosses, he offered to "see no evil" in exchange for a percentage of their illicit earnings.

His first real swindle was carried out in 1890, and it was a classic: he went door to door selling the miraculous *Meriwether's Elixir*, cure for parasites of all shapes and sizes. The main ingredient of the medicine? Rainwater.

Joseph Weil, November 11th, 1974, under arrest.

Ingenious Innovator

From then on, nothing seemed to slow down the Yellow Kid's explosive rise to fame and fortune. Or, almost nothing. Weil was at heart a gentlemen: a latter-day Robin Hood, his personal sense of "professional" ethics led him to dupe only the "dishonest" rich, and to always leave his victims with enough to "start over" and get back on their feet.

> *I never took everything they had. I always left them enough to survive. Never send them to the river – that was my motto.*

An elegant man, in a tailored suit and silk shirt, Weil always presented a reassuring image, allowing him to pass now for a banker, now for an oil tycoon, now for whatever his indefatigable imagination suggested to him, wherever he detected the prospect of a profitable piece of business.

It was human greed above all that he used as a lever in his ingenious schemes. Like when he groomed a stray dog and casually mentioned to a bartender that it was a rare pedigree breed. He then entrusted the dog to the man on some pretext for a few hours and observed contentedly as the primed mechanism clicked into action: an accomplice of Weil would enter the premises, recognize the "valuable" animal, and offer the bartender a considerable sum for it. The disingenuous bartender, believing he could profit from the situation, would then tell the man that he'd like to think it over, and that maybe he should call back later. But a short time later, a "depressed" Weil would come back to the bar, claiming that he had just lost a lot of money in a deal that fell through. The bartender (taking the bait) would offer to help by buying the dog – obviously for a lot less than he expected to make selling it to the other man. Reluctantly, Weil would agree, accepting the offer, taking the bartender's money, and leaving the aspiring speculator with a stray mutt and great expectations.

A chap who wants something for nothing usually winds up with nothing for something.

Chickens to Be Plucked

Countless scams have been attributed to the legendary figure of the Yellow Kid, such as the sale of a bite-sized piece of chicken for the price of a gold nugget (a transaction memorialized today, according to the legend, by "chicken nuggets"). Not least of his successes was the swindling of Benito Mussolini, who bought a two million dollar mining concession on a non-existent property in Colorado.

The strategy of the con artist is based on an infallible premise: if the mark, or victim, is a willing accomplice in an illegal act – such as trying to sell a worthless dog for a hundred dollars – then he can't report the fraud without revealing his own guilt.

ONE NAME FOR A THOUSAND FACES

Various legends circulate about how Joseph Weil came to have his curious nickname. Very little, apart from their modest origins, links the chameleon impostor to Mickey Dugan, the bald urchin with the protruding teeth invented by Richard F. Outcault in 1894. "It was said that it was due to my having worn yellow chamois gloves, yellow vests, yellow spats, and a yellow beard. All this was untrue. I had never affected such wearing apparel and I had no beard," declared Weil. The most likely explanation is that it was the result of his collaboration with a certain Frank Hogan. By associating Hogan with a popular, late nineteenth-century comic strip, Hogan's Alley, Weil picked up the name of the strip's main character, the Yellow Kid. But this is perhaps a far too plain explanation for such an imaginative man.

This same strategy is at work in the case of an old gentleman involved in a clandestine boxing competition: betting on what he sees as a sure win, the gentlemen, at the sudden "death" of one of the contestants, flees in panic, leaving the stake he bet on the encounter to his swindlers.

A Question of Trust

The infinite tricks of the Yellow Kid reveal a lot about human nature. People are disposed to believe in anything that promises them some advantage. For example: a fellow meets a stranger in a bar. The stranger has this opportunity of a lifetime. He'll give the fellow a plot of land merely for the pleasure of having him as a neighbor. So the fellow packs his things and moves out there. Only then does he realize that his longed for Garden of Eden is in reality worth less than the exorbitant bureaucratic costs demanded for the move. This standard scheme, repeated in many places, filled the pockets of Weil and his accomplices for years. The victims, brought face to face with their own vanity, could do no more than try and salve their wounded pride: the strategy was unassailable.

The term "confidence man" describes a person who gains the trust of the victim in order to lead them into a trap: the victim enters willingly. It was no accident that Weil chose Fred Buckminster as his accomplice, a man who he himself described as having "the most innocent face you ever saw. Looking at him you would have sworn that he could not be anything but honest." Nicknamed "The Deacon," Buckminster was a policeman who abandoned the way of the law for the more profitable way of the swindler.

With his help, Weil staged massive productions, such as renting the offices vacated by a bank and setting up his own temporary credit institution, with "units" and "extras" recruited from the circuit of the deceit professionals. Their prey, attracted by the mirage of solid financial investment opportunities in the midst of the chaos of the Great Depression, and taken in by the mountains of overflowing bags of money cast about the place, and by the busy hive of customers and employees hurrying to and fro, couldn't wait to invest their cash savings.

The success of my schemes was due largely to the build-up. [...] In some cases the build-up was so convincing that nothing could shake the victim's confidence in me.

His sensational career was said to have yielded approximately 8 million dollars in all (offset by only six years in jail), money which he squandered extravagantly over his hundred-year lifetime. Buying what he could and selling what he did not have, Weil became the owner of buildings, banks, horses, land, mines, and oil fields. It mattered little if this was fact or fiction. When the Yellow Kid blew out his hundredth candle, in 1975, he was poor, but still full of energy and eager as always to set up another trick.

The Captain
of Köpenick

Friedrich Wilhelm Voigt (Germany)

A shoe-maker with a criminal record found himself in an absurd situation: he couldn't get a job because he didn't have a passport and he couldn't get a passport because he didn't have a job. Exasperated, he got his revenge on the State by masquerading as an officer, pulling off a sensational swindle that mocked and exposed the contradictions and formal manners of Prussian society.

If an army captain commanding a substantial escort of soldiers bursts into a town hall, declares the burgomaster and the treasurer under arrest for administrative irregularities, and confiscates the town treasury, leaving a countersigned receipt for it – it is unlikely that any witness would suspect that the thief is not the unlucky burgomaster but the officer who has just handcuffed him. In cases like this one, the observer of the scene is instinctively on the side of the men in uniform, even if these people are strangers. And thus a brilliant criminal, Friedrich Wilhelm Voigt, managed to get his hands on 4000 marks. It happened on October 16th, 1906, in Köpenick, a few years before this postcard town just outside Berlin, looking onto the River Spree and deep in the woods, was absorbed by the inexorable expansion of the German capital.

Victim of a Paradox

Life in Prussia in the second half of the nineteenth century could be very hard. While Bismarck and Kaiser Wilhelm I were building the German Empire, the lower social strata were condemned to exploitation and practically unbearable living conditions. Berlin was trying to achieve the appearance of a great European capital, but the density of its population was the highest in Europe. In the enormous, quickly and cheaply constructed apartment blocks, buildings crammed with ex-artisans and ex-peasants drawn to the city by new industries, diseases, alcoholism and crime spread rapidly. But every form of social protest, and every possibility of rebellion had to reckon with the omnipresent army and police. Things were no different in provincial cities.

Wilhelm Voigt, born into a family of shoe-makers on February 13th, 1849, in Tilsit, far in the east of Prussia, was arrested for the first time at fourteen. He was immediately convicted of theft. In the following years, he wandered from city to city, searching for work, and trying various more or less legal expedients to make ends meet. But, for petty crimes, from theft to forging checks, he achieved only notoriety with the police.

Mugshot of Friedrich Wilhelm Voigt.

In 1890, he designed a plan to seize the treasury of the courthouse in the town of Wongrowitz. When the "job" failed, Voigt was sentenced to fifteen years in prison and forced labor. Released in February of 1906, he intended to make an honest living.

He was appalled to discover, however, that, even free, he was still in some ways a prisoner: he found himself trapped in one of those Kafkaesque bureaucratic short circuits which can ruin the life of a citizen with no friends in high places. When he knocked on doors looking for work, he was asked to show his passport or residence permit: without these, no one offered him a regular post. But since Voigt was an ex-prisoner, he didn't have a residence permit: according to the law, only with a stable residence could one apply for such a permit. But, in order to obtain residence in the city, he needed a job, and therefore a passport. On August 24th, 1906, the situation became even more ridiculous. Due to his criminal record and practically homeless condition, Voigt was officially expelled from Berlin. But in order to leave Prussia, in search of better fortune . . . he needed a passport.

A Question of Identity

With the law a mockery, Voigt began to think of obtaining, in his own way, not only a passport but also sensational revenge on the State. If the authorities prevented him from affirming his identity, he would give himself another, and not just any identity, but that of the enemy, one of those watchdogs in uniform who had always been breathing down his neck.

From second-hand shops and flea markets he acquired all the elements of an officer's uniform, and then practiced wearing the uniform with assurance and ease. He tested his credibility by walking in front of soldiers, who saluted him respectfully.

In October, he was ready to put his plan into action: he made for the military post at Plötzensee. Then, at the shooting range, he ordered two garrisoned squads of grenadiers to follow him. And since Prussian soldiers, like most soldiers, tend to obey an officer's orders without question, they did. Voigt and his men were on the next train for Köpenick. When they got off, they marched in tight formation for the Rathaus, the town hall. At this point, Voigt completely identified with the part he had assigned himself. He ordered the soldiers to block the exits to the building and to cut communications with Berlin. Then he went in, arrested the burgomaster, Georg Langerhans, together with the treasurer, August von Wiltberg, and ordered his soldiers to take the prisoners to the capital to be interrogated. He searched the offices for a blank passport – planning on filling it out with

A BELOVED BURGOMASTER

After Voigt's arrest, the burgomaster Georg Langerhans resigned from his position. The shame of being fooled was too great. Most humiliating was being asked to explain, at the interrogation, how he could have "swallowed" the fake captain's hook, how he could have handed over the keys to the treasury and let himself be arrested without even inspecting the arrest warrant – what's more, he was a man of the law!

In the end, the judges were understanding. Voigt had tricked many other people, as well, including the eleven grenadiers who had obeyed his orders without question. In fact, the judges persuaded Langerhans to withdraw his resignation and remain in office. The residents of Köpenick were even more sympathetic: in 1915, they re-elected Langerhans as burgomaster.

his personal data – but he didn't find one. So he forced von Wiltberg to hand over the city treasury. Then, after giving orders to his men to remain in Köpenick and guard the town hall, Voigt went off alone. At the station, he put on civilian clothes and, with 4000 marks in his pockets, vanished into thin air.

Unexpected Fame

It took the soldiers (and the whole town) some time to realize that something wasn't right. The captain was not coming back. But by then, the man was long gone.

The police were not as clueless. They immediately identified the suspect and within ten days had Friedrich Wilhelm Voigt behind bars once again. In the meantime, however, the mysterious officer who had fooled everyone had become a popular hero. His exploit, half swindle and half Dadaist performance before its time, between illegal appropriation and public protest against an insensitive, militaristic system, was given a lot of space in the German and international press. However, it was in the beer houses, cabarets, factories, and the local theaters that the "Captain of Köpenick" myth was born: four days after Voigt's arrest, the wax museum in Berlin already had a statue of Voigt on display.

The public opinion in his favor ended up affecting the judges. Voigt's sentence was light, considering his criminal record. Even then, there was so much talk about the man that in 1908 the Kaiser decided to issue a pardon.

Once released, the Captain of Köpenick began to exploit his popularity by signing autographs and telling his tale in theaters. He even published a book, *How I Became the Captain of Köpe-*

ON THE STAGE AND ON FILM

Voigt's show was certainly not the only one devoted to the character of the Captain of Köpenick, who over the years inspired many artists and directors, not only in Germany.

Among the most successful were Carl Zuckmayer's theatrical comedy *Der Hauptmann von Köpenick* (1931) ("The Captain of Köpenick," adapted into English by John Mortimer in 1971) and the films *The Captain of Koepenick* ("I was a Criminal") by Richard Oswald, with Albert Bassermann, shot in 1941, and *Der Hauptmann von Köpenick* by Helmut Käutner, with Heinz Rühmann (1956), which received an Oscar nomination.

nick. His fame, however, ended up irritating the authorities, who forbade him from appearing in public. But Voigt was not a man to give up easily. He invented a way to tell his tale without breaking the letter of the law, again mocking the rigidity of the institution: he gave no more lectures or interviews, but toured Germany interpreting "The Captain of Köpenick" in a comedic reconstruction of his exploit. By acting, he had pretended to be an officer in order to obtain a passport, and through acting he then managed to recover a respectable identity. And he did this without needing to show his documents.

Stealing the Mona Lisa

Vincenzo Peruggia (France)

In 1911, Leonardo da Vinci's masterpiece was stolen from the Louvre. The thief, it was eventually determined, was either a poor Italian emigrant, or a man who claimed to be an Argentinian marquis. His motive? Patriotism, or perhaps, more prosaically, money. In fact, with the painting missing, a fake *Mona Lisa* circulating on the market could be passed off as the original. Thus begins one of the most thrilling mysteries in the world of art, which more than a century later still remains unsolved, and which begs an important question: Is the *Mona Lisa* on display today the real one?

The theft of the *Mona Lisa* from the Louvre on Monday, August 21st, 1911, is a crime story with a plot as complex as a game of Chinese boxes. Despite all the ink spilt on the subject, and perhaps because of this, many questions remain unanswered. Who actually stole the painting? Why? Who planned the heist? And where – as some people still ask – did the "real" *Mona Lisa* end up? In fact, the mystery surrounding this century-old crime is just one of many in the history of this work. Historians and critics, beginning with Vasari, have discussed for 500 years who Leonardo's female (or male!) model was, where the landscape was portrayed in the painting's background, and what the original work looked like, since its creator continued to modify it over the years. Not to mention the woman's enigmatic smile. To muddy the waters even more, there are copies of the work, at least two dozen from various eras, some contemporary with the first *Mona Lisa* (which was probably begun in 1503) which could be the work of Leonardo himself. The painting raises a series of fascinating questions, all of which have contributed to the myth of the *Mona Lisa*, making it the most famous painting in the world.

Monday, August 21st, 1911

The most probable sequence of events, supported by the testimony given during proceedings of the trial, is the following. The thief was a man named Vincenzo Peruggia, from Dumenza, not far from Lake Maggiore on the Italian-Swiss border. He emigrated to France in 1907. With a diploma in decoration and design, he was hired by one of the painters working in the Louvre. Peruggia himself might have been given the task of cleaning the *Mona Lisa* and enclosing it in a glass case.

The actual theft was incredibly simple. Peruggia chose to act on a Monday, when the museum was closed for cleaning and mainte-

An official photo for the recovery of the Mona Lisa after its theft in 1911.

Mug shot and fingerprints of Vincenzo Peruggia.

nance. He knew the museum well, and very early in the morning passed the concierge, who was dozing, and headed straight for the Salon Carré, where Leonardo's masterpiece was hanging between a Giorgione and a Correggio. He took down the painting, removed the crystal glass and the frame, which would later be found on the floor above, wrapped the wooden panel of the *Mona Lisa* in his jacket – it was small, 30 x 21 inches, but not easy to carry – and left the museum by a tortuous route, via multiple staircases, service doors, and secondary courtyards. Once outside, he boarded a bus, realized he was going in the wrong direction, got off and hurriedly took a taxi home, an attic in Rue de l'Hôpital Saint-Louis. There he hid the painting in a hidden compartment in the kitchen table and hurriedly returned to the Louvre, where he began his shift. It was a true Fantomas performance, carried out by the least professional of thieves.

For the Louvre and the whole of France, the theft of the *Mona Lisa* was a real shock, a blow *inimaginable*, to quote the newspaper headlines. The police took the fingerprints of all 257 employees of the Louvre, checked the movements of 1350 suspects, and even interrogated Peruggia and searched his attic, without finding anything. The police completed paperwork on the very table inside of which the poor *Mona Lisa* looked up at them. For weeks, there were frenetic investigations: even Picasso was a suspect, and detained by the police, and Guillaume Apollinaire ended up in jail for ten days. But the painting could not be found. Time passed, and soon enough it was assumed that the painting was already in America, in the hands of some collector. Others suspected a German plot against France.

A UNIVERSAL ICON

The *Mona Lisa* has always been a painting enchanting to copyists, who see in it the highest qualities of Renaissance art. In every aspect, from the position of the hands, to the background, to the famous smile, da Vinci's work offers material for endless hours of study. From a marketing point of view, as well, the *Mona Lisa* is a universal icon, which could be described as pop. Millions of copies have been reproduced in every shape and form: breakfast mugs, fridge magnets, T-shirts, puzzles. For artists, the painting has always been a source of inspiration, and this justifies the numerous "authentic copies" present in museums, like the *Monna Lisa Anteriore* preserved in Geneva, or the St. Petersburg Gioconda, which is thought to be in a private collection. In 2012, the Prado museum presented the restoration of the oldest copy of the *Monna Lisa*, which was probably done between 1503 and 1516 by one of da Vinci's pupils.

Then, one afternoon two years later, Vincenzo Peruggia read an advertisement by a Florence gallery-owner, Alfredo Geri, who was looking for valuable pictures for an exhibition. Peruggia wrote to Geri, introducing himself as Vincent Léonard, and the two of them arranged to meet in a Florence hotel (a place called the "Gioconda" – the other name of the *Mona Lisa* – ever since). Taking the train from Paris, Peruggia brought the *Mona Lisa* wrapped in dirty linen. Geri turned up for the appointment accompanied by the director of the Uffizi, Giovanni Poggi, who, after seeing the painting, asked to keep it in order to examine it. The next day, the naïve Peruggia was arrested, and in 1914 the stolen painting was returned to the Louvre on a special train, the arrival of which was met by the president of the Republic and other members of the government.

The trial took place in Florence. Peruggia was sentenced to a little more than a year in prison, but this was reduced on appeal to seven months. Such a light sentence was justified by the motive for the theft: patriotism. As Peruggia's daughter, Celestina (nicknamed "Giocondina"), related in an interview given shortly before her death in 2011, her father was not inspired by money, but by a desire to recover for Italy what France had stolen:

> *First, he thought that the painting was Napoleon's booty. Second, he wanted to mock the French who had laughed at his mandolin playing, or called him scornfully "the macaroni-eater." He denied wanting to become rich by selling the Mona Lisa to dishonest art merchants.*

This was arguable, given that the painting was not the fruit of Napoleonic spoliation, but had been sold by Leonardo himself to King Francis I of France; and that Peruggia had already tried to sell the painting to a British merchant, even traveling to London to do so. In any case, after the trial, the ex-painter became a popular hero.

Another Version: Swindle

In 1932, the journalist Karl Decker, in the *Saturday Evening Post*, gave a second, completely contrasting, account of the theft. Decker's tale was about a swindle. According to Decker, a self-proclaimed Argentinian marquis, Eduardo de Valfierno, commissioned a famous forger, Yves Chaudron, in 1910 to make six copies of the *Mona Lisa*, planning to send them abroad in the expectation of profitable sales. The disappearance of the original from the Louvre would help him to sell the forgeries at the highest price. In fact, Valfierno revealed to an interviewer that he sold a copy of the painting for 300,000 dollars. In Decker's account, Peruggia was only the inside man in a band of thieves. Unfortunately, Decker, who was already notorious for his use of unreliable sources, couldn't substantiate his claims: when he interviewed Valfierno, who no one apart from the journalist knew about, both Chaudron and Peruggia were dead. Nonetheless, the hypothesis of the existence of these six forgeries has persisted. Even if nobody has ever seen them, many believe there is an element of truth to Decker's tale.

And so other versions of the theft have piled up over time, vastly inflating the currency of "*Mona Lisa* trafficking" stories. In one of these, the Florentine gallery-owner Geri plays a part: piqued by the miserliness of the reward given him by France (a check for 25 francs), he is said to have returned a forgery, keeping the original for himself. Thus, according to this version, the Mona Lisa is presently in Florence. But where, exactly?

The World, the Flesh and the Devil

Horatio Bottomley (United Kingdom)

From the orphanage to extreme poverty via Westminster, the *Financial Times*, and 67 counts of bankruptcy: in the world of swindlers, Horatio Bottomley is very famous. He is rarely absent from the literature. Some consider him among the greatest of con men. But in examining this figure, we find more quantity than quality. He lacks the depth, the stroke of genius, the vision, the elegance – not in dress but in his actions – of many of his peers. In short, for all his popularity, perhaps Bottomley was just an overblown barker, a run-of-the-mill serial swindler. Perhaps.

Let's begin in 1914, when Bottomley carefully searched all of Europe for a low-profile, remote race track. He wanted to commit the perfect crime.

He chose Blankenberge, in Belgium, 9.5 miles from Bruges and 12.5 miles from Ostend, on the North Sea. Blankenberge had a seaside resort, and it was known that it drew a relaxed, easy going and middle-class crowd. Furthermore, the Blankenberge track was surrounded by high sand dunes. Part of the track, in fact, was hidden behind a dune, and out of view of the stands. In short, it was the ideal location. Six horses were in the race. Bottomley owned all of them; he'd bought them for this particular purpose. The jockeys, too, were all British, all on his payroll. Bottomley decided the finishing positions beforehand: first place to sixth. He enlisted a number of visitors to the track that day to bet enormous sums (of Bottomley's money, of course) on those positions.

Horatio Bottomley: a posed photo from 1920.

But on the day of the race, the fog was so thick that the jockeys couldn't see or hear each other on the track. The result was fortuitous, though completely different from what Bottomley had planned.

The man lost everything. Meaning: he lost *a lot*.

The Hansard Union

Or else we could relate the Hansard Publishing Union, a publishing house with wide horizons founded in 1889 by Bottomley with a high-profile board of directors. On the board were, among others, the Mayor of London, various lords, and well-known entrepreneurs. Bottomley proposed the purchase of printing factories, land, and offices – also abroad. Not to worry:

JOHN BULL

In 1906, Bottomley published a periodical, *John Bull*. He took the title from a nineteenth-century jingoist publication. Jingoism was a school of thought and a movement, that promoted chauvinist, racist, and nationalist views, and that advocated a violent, substantially war-mongering foreign policy.

In the United Kingdom, the first to describe a political view as *jingoist* was George Holyoake, in 1878. It was no accident that Holyoake, a secularist and well-known agitator, was Bottomley's maternal grandfather.

The social movement Holyoake, with Charles Bradlaugh (another eminent figure who encouraged the young Bottomley to enter politics) helped organize would achieve, or contribute to achieving, important victories for the British working class: they fought for fair working hours, pensions, and the right to form cooperatives. But both were fundamentally populists and demagogues.

John Bull was the synthesis of this ideological and pragmatic confusion, a forum for Bottomley's political views.

he would negotiate the deals himself. In fact, by using various figureheads, he skimmed the company on the purchases. (Incidentally, quite a few of these ventures flopped.) In practice, he spent 200,000 pounds setting up several printing business, only to quickly sell these to his partners for 325,000 pounds. He added to this little tip of 125,000 pounds the 75,000 pounds he took from the company to buy a publishing house in Austria, that he would never purchase.

After their first year in business, the balance sheet of the Union was completely red. Still, Bottomley paid a dividend of 8%, issuing bonds valued at 50,000 pounds. In 1891, the Union was not able to redeem the bonds and failed. In the trial that followed, it emerged that Bottomley had embezzled 100,000 pounds (almost a million pounds today, or 1.5 million dollars). It was unclear what actually happened to this money. There should have been no doubt at the trial, but Bottomley's oratory (he defended himself), added to weaknesses in the prosecution, led to a verdict of acquittal.

A Finger in Every Pie

Bottomley was a businessman, and spent most of his career in publishing. Although many of the publishing houses he started failed, he also had a hand in the creation of the *Financial Times.*

Bottomley was a patriot. During the First World War, he would organize nearly 300 demonstrations throughout Great Britain to recruit soldiers, incite hate against the Germans, and to keep the morale of the country high. These were epic events.

Bottomley was a fervid patriot and a great orator. It would become known years later that, in many cases, he asked to be paid for the demonstrations he organized and spoke at, and that, all in all, he earned about 80,000 pounds during the war. Bottomley was a dealmaker who loved risk. In 1889, he opened a company that sold stock in Australian gold mines. The mines were real, and produced as mines should, but Bottomley's company sold the same stock several, even five or six times. Bottomley used the profits from this operation to repay the debts from the failure of the Union. It was a pity that some debtors were paid in stock that had already been sold several times, and thus were worthless.

Bottomley was a politician. He served in Parliament twice, once for the Liberals (1906-1912), and once as an independent (1918-1921). In both cases, his career was brusquely terminated by convictions for fraud. The first concerned the mine-stock scandal. The second came to be known as the Victory Bonds scandal.

He was a polarizing figure, but it could not be said that Bottomley's views as a businessman were inconsistent with his politics. In his manifesto, he wrote that the government should be composed of businessmen, not politicians.

Bottomley was a consistent politician. When the war started, he said to his assistant:

This war is my opportunity. Whatever I have been in the past, and whatever my faults, I am going to draw a line at August 4th, 1914, and start afresh. I shall play the game, cut my all old associates, and wipe out everything pre-1914.

Bottomley was a journalist. In his life he contributed to many publications. Everything he wrote was aimed at either promoting his career or destroying those of his opponents, using often uncharitable comments. One time he dedicated an entire article

A LITTLE GOSSIP AND THE END

To sum up: his maternal grandfather was George Holyoake. Charles Bradlaugh was Holyoake's right-hand man in political struggles (together they founded the National Republican League) and obviously visited his home. Elizabeth Holyoake, George's daughter, was Horatio Bottomley's mother. Horatio's father was a man named William; he was mentally disturbed. Horatio was born in London on March 23rd, 1860. Very soon it was observed that Horatio bore a striking resemblance to Charles Bradlaugh. As an adult, Horatio allowed the rumors to circulate. He did nothing to stop them – in fact, the contrary was true.

Bottomley had a difficult childhood. William died when Horatio was four; Elizabeth died the next year. Horatio spent a few years with one uncle or another, and then ended up in an orphanage for five years. He was fourteen when he got out.

As an adult, Bottomley lived in luxury, with oysters and champagne. In 1880, he married a woman named Eliza Norton. Actually, they had planned on marrying the year before, but at the last moment Bottomley lost everything on some bets, and so they were forced to postpone the marriage. Eliza lived for long periods in their house in Monte Carlo. In general, Bottomley was considered driven, not only for money and power, but for sex. In fact, he kept numerous lovers available in different cities. It was once noted of him:

He preferred them to be shapely, short, blonde, and from a working-class family.

In 1930, after yet another business failure, Eliza died, and soon afterward Horatio was evicted by the son-in-law from his great property in Sussex, where he had lived for over seventy years. Every penny he put into the place, some said, was bilked.

Only an old lover remained by his side. And when he was broke, alone, poor, forgotten, and finished, she offered him shelter in her home. Peggy Primrose was a starlet in her day, and, when he had the means, Bottomley had tried to launch her into show business. Horatio Bottomley died in a hospital, perhaps in her arms, on May 26th, 1933.

to a fellow Member of Parliament, concluding that the man was "the illegitimate son of a Scottish servant." His most famous column was called:

The World, the Flesh and the Devil.

Bottomley, inexplicably, by a supernatural stroke of luck, could not be arrested. Even following bankruptcy, personal complaints and vendettas, business failures, countless times in court, the man was untouchable.

Finally, the Victory Bonds

At the end of the Great War, the British government offered Victory Bonds to finance postwar recovery. One bond sold for 5 pounds; the rate of interest was 5% and the maturity term of one year.

Bottomley announced that he wanted to help less well-off families, people for whom 5 pounds was too high a figure. So he created the Victory Bonds Club. The Club bought bonds on behalf of its members, who in this way could invest any amount of money, even one shilling. Since Bottomley was still respected among the British proletariat, in a few years he collected 900,000 pounds in micro-investments. As usual, he kept a gratuity for himself. This amounted to around 150,000 pounds (thus the umpteenth trial would declare, in 1922) and he used the money to pay his debts, buy champagne, seduce lovers, buy horses, gamble, extend the garden of his Sussex estate, and (for 15,000 pounds) buy a German submarine – just to show his friends.

This time, Bottomley was caught. He was sentenced to seven years. He served four and was then released on parole. He came out a shell of the man he was.

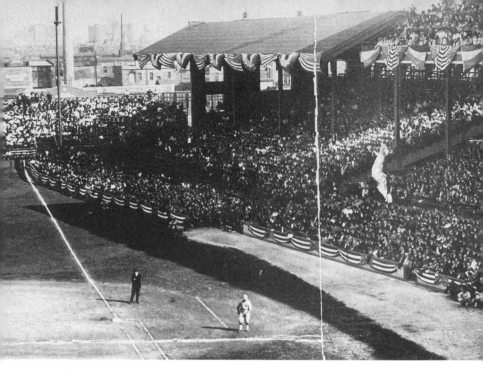

The Curse
of the Black Sox

Chick Gandil, Eddie Cicotte and others
(United States)

In the 1919 World Series, the Chicago White Sox faced the unpopular Cincinnati Reds. The outcome seemed a foregone conclusion. Everyone was ready, that October 1st, to greet the most celebrated champions of America's national sport. Except that, some days before, in a hotel room in New York . . .

On the evening of September 21st, 1919, Chick Gandil, first base for the Chicago White Sox, met his friend Joseph "Sport" Sullivan, a bookie, in the Ansonia Hotel. Other players for the Sox joined them: Happy Felsch, Buck Weaver, Fred McMullin, the rude Swede Risberg, and the pitchers, Lefty Williams and Eddie Cicotte. Williams and Cicotte were indispensable in fixing the outcome of the game, because in baseball the pitchers have the most control over how and when to make offensive plays. Cicotte was in enormous financial difficulties: he'd recently bought a small farm, but he wasn't able to make his mortgage payments. Joe Jackson, the best hitter on the team, though absent, had been informed of the matter, his companions assure Sullivan. He, along with the seven co-conspirators in the room that night, would come to be known in the aftermath of the scandal as one of the Black Sox.

It was ten days from the first game. After a night of argument, the players told Sullivan that they would throw the series in exchange for 10,000 dollars a head. Sullivan said it would be difficult to get that kind of money together in such a short time, but that he would do what he could.

The issue was complicated. Two other bookies, Bill Burns and Billy Maharg, came to hear of the deal, and approached Gandil and Cicotte with an offer of 100,000 dollars. They also said that they would manage the swindle, deciding which games to manipulate. Then Burns and Maharg went to New York to meet the undisputed Number One in the field of illegal betting, Arnold Rothstein. But Rothstein was at a horse race, so they were received by the chief's right-hand man, Abe Attell, former featherweight boxing champion of the world. Inexplicably, Rothstein said he was not interested. He was skeptical. At least, that's what Attell had Burns and Maharg believe.

Corrupt Players and Unscrupulous Punters

In those years, players were easily tempted: Jackson and Weaver, the stars of the Chicago White Sox – which had been the national

Players on the field during the World Series of 1919, in a match between Chicago White Sox and Cincinnati Reds.

champion just two years before – earned 6000 dollars a year. The money offered by the bookies was obviously hard to resist. Moreover, in this specific event, the owner of the team, Charles Comiskey, had a reputation of being a stingy miser. It is said that the name "Black Sox," which the 1919 scandal would be remembered as, referred to the fact that, tired of paying the cleaners, the players had ended up not washing their uniforms. Soaked with sweat and dust, the uniforms had slowly changed color, from their original white to a dark gray. Comiskey, exasperated, ordered the players wash them. But at their own expense.

The team was divided along a philosophical, if not ethical, line. One side scarcely spoke to the other, on or off the field. The more dissatisfied contingent, and the group more inclined to try to earn money on the side, were Gandil and his co-conspirators. Sullivan, meanwhile, had raised half the money, 40,000 dollars. However, instead of giving it to the players, who he thought could wait a few more days, he bet 30,000 dollars on the Cincinnati Reds, whose odds were plummeting, and gave 10,000 dollars to Gandil. The first baseman put the money under the pillow of the pitcher of the first game, Cicotte (who, not knowing where to hide it in a rush, sewed it inside the lining of his jacket).

Having only received a small part of the money that had been promised, the Black Sox then turned to Abe Attell. They met in Cincinnati, at the Sinton Hotel, on September 30th, 1919, on the eve of the first of potentially nine games. There Attell agreed to give them 20,000 dollars for every defeat. As guarantor, he offered no less than the name of Rothstein. In reality, the initiative was Attell's alone. His boss was in the dark. Or so it seemed.

The Chicago White Sox vs. the Cincinnati Reds

The following day, there wasn't a single open seat on the bleachers of Redland Field in Cincinnati. Scalpers were asking 50 dollars a ticket, a record figure. At the Ansonia Hotel, hundreds of people – among them Arnold Rothstein – were in the hall, where a speaker was ready to give a commentary on every play. A large cardboard reproduction of the field, complete with little figures, was set up. All was ready.

The amount of money bet on the underdog team in the preceding days had aroused a lot of suspicion. For this reason Hugh Fullerton, a journalist for the *Chicago Herald and Examiner,* decided to record every unusual play. He did not have long to wait. Cicotte's second pitch: he hit the batter, an agreed signal. The game – a "terrifying blow," *The New York Times* reported the next day – was a slaughter. The Reds: 9 to 1. Game two was a little better: 4-2, the Reds. Then Bill Burns, working for Attell, delivered 10,000 dollars (half of what was promised) to Gandil. But Gandil couldn't keep his team-mates in line: they were angry at not having received what had been agreed. Then the White Sox, before a home crowd, dominated the following game: 3-0. Sullivan intervened a few hours before the fourth game, giving 5000 dollars to Jackson and Williams: 2-0 for the Reds, because of two errors by Cicotte in the fifth inning. Game five went the same way. The Reds: 5 to 0. Cicotte was making elementary pitching errors. Fullerton noted two other errors by Happy Felsch, writing in the margin of his notebook: "Why'd he ever do it?" The Reds led the series 4 games to 1: they needed only one more victory to clinch the final.

A Conspiracy. But the Money?

Gandil and companions, not having received the agreed sums, decided not to keep their side of the bargain. They played for the White Sox to win. And that's what happened: Chicago won game six, 5 to 4. Then they won game seven, 4 to 1, bringing the series to 4 games to 3. But for the criminal organizations involved, it was no joke. Lefty Williams, the White Sox pitcher for next game, received a visit from a notorious gangster, Harry F., who set things straight. Williams played so badly that he was benched. Cincinnati won the game 10-5, and took the series title.

Something strange had happened. Rumors of a fix were rife, but the baseball league closed ranks, denying every accusation. Even Comiskey rebuffed the suggestion. The image of the White Sox and professional baseball could not be sullied by admitting that the outcome of the series had been decided off the field by betting syndicates. Too much money was involved.

The National Sport Transformed into a Swindle

However, a few months later the first admissions began to emerge. In July of the following year the White Sox trainer, Kid Gleason, met Abe Attell in a bar in New York. Allegedly, Attell remarked: "You know, I hate to say it. But I knew that I would make a bag of money. And there was nothing I could do about it." Some weeks later, in an interview published in Philadelphia's *The North American*, Maharg revealed every detail of the swindle. Then, on September 28th, Cicotte was the first to admit his guilt. In tears, he said:

> *I do not know why I did it, I must have been crazy. I needed money. [...] I should not have done it even for a million dollars. I have lost everything, job, reputation, everything.*

Then Jackson, Williams, and Felsch confessed in turn. It was as if they had to get that weight off their conscience. On October 22nd, 1920, a Grand Jury indicted eight White Sox players and five bookies, including Sullivan (who escaped to Mexico) and Attell (who escaped to Canada), on nine counts of fraud and for damaging the interests of the league and of the same Comiskey. Rothstein was not indicted. He was never accused by anyone, and there was no evidence against him. Rumors, of course, circulated, suggesting that he was the one pulling the strings of the entire operation. But Rothstein was untouchable.

Appointment in Court

Before the trial began on June 27th, 1921, the depositions and the admissions of guilt of the players disappeared completely. On the first day of the trial, all eight accused players were present, but not the bookies. George Gorman, for the prosecution, found a key witness in Maharg. He tracked down Bill Burns, who was fishing in Texas. In exchange for assurances of immunity, Burns agreed to testify. The defense, in turn, called Kid Gleason to the stand: in a key statement, the Sox trainer claimed that his players were practicing in front of his very eyes at the time Burns was supposed to have met them.

In his closing argument, Edward Prindeville, Gorman's assistant, was emphatic and passionate:

> *They have taken in the spectators, the owners of the teams, even the children who play on the little fields. The culprits have taken our national sport and they have transformed it into a swindle.*

However, it was a question put to the jury by the defense that hit the bullseye: "Why has Arnold Rothstein not been indicted? Why, instead, have they brought here underpaid players and two-bit bookies, who at most would have made nickels and dimes? Because they were sacrificed as scapegoats."

On August 3rd, all of the accused were acquitted, triggering scenes of exultation in the courtroom, with players and spectators cheering and embracing. Their joy was to be short-lived.

As You Make Your Bed . . .

The next morning, it was announced that eight players for the Chicago White Sox were banned from future competition. In-

THE CURSE OF THE BLACK SOX

Once disqualified, some players tried to organize an exhibition tour, but they had to back down when Landis threatened to publicly ban anyone from baseball that participated in it. Some played in the minor league under different names: a pathetic come-down for someone who had once had a shining career at the top.

In Francis Scott Fitzgerald's 1925 novel, *The Great Gatsby*, a minor character named Meyer Wolfsheim, whose name recalls Arnold Rothstein, claims to have taken part in the 1919 World Series fixing.

In Francis Ford Coppola's *The Godfather: Part II* (1974), the boss Hyman Roth states that he's loved baseball since "Arnold Rothstein rigged the World Series in 1919." Whether Rothstein had a hand in the scandal has never been determined, although it is clear that he knew about the fix and that as he wagered, in fact, something like 400,000 dollars on the Cincinnati Reds.

Eighty-six years would pass before the Chicago team won the title again, in 2005, giving credence to what came to be known as "The Curse of the Black Sox".

cluded in this decision was Buck Weaver, who had not taken a dime and who had played an impeccable final series. His crime? Remaining silent. Joc Jackson was also banned. He had batted magnificently (hitting the only out-of-the-park run) and hadn't made a single error: but he had played to make things look good for the bookies, and then had been unable to refuse the money they offered him.

The official statement of the new president of the league, Kenesaw Landis, was a benchmark decision: "No player who has intentionally committed a game error, or who has taken part in secret meetings with corrupt teammates or bookmakers and who has not reported such conspiracies immediately to his manager, will never play a professional game of baseball again."

Happy Felsch, in the *Chicago American*, summed up the effects of this decision in a few words:

> *I got 5000 dollars, more or less what I would have earned if the White Sox had won the series. Now I am out of baseball, the only work that I am able to do, while many bookmakers have become rich. It looks like we are the losers in the end.*

In the end, many aspects of the whole story are incomprehensible, ambiguous, mysterious: there were multiple spontaneous confessions, disqualifications associated with the acquittals, evidence that disappeared, and suspects never charged . . .

Habes Lector candide fortiss. ac inuictiss Dycis Draeck ad viuum imaginem
toto terrarum orbe, suorum omnium, et mensium decem spatio, Zephiris sauen-
tibus circumducto. Anglain sedes preprius, 4 Cal Octobr. anno a partu Virg
nis 1520 reuisit cum antea portu soluisset Jil. Decem. anni .1577

Drake's Treasure

Oscar Hartzell (United States)

In the 1920s and 1930s, Oscar Hartzell, a farmer from Iowa, set up a complex scam based on secrecy and the get-rich-quick illusion. Hartzell promised, to anyone who made a "donation" to his endeavor, a share in the fabulous inheritance of Sir Francis Drake, the English explorer who died in the Caribbean in 1596. The inheritance, naturally, did not exist. But tens of thousands of investors thought otherwise. For over fifteen years, Hartzell accepted money from people willing to chase the dream of finding lost "pirate treasure."

He was a dangerous outlaw, a valorous commander, a common murderer, and one of the great English patriots. He was an explorer, a politician, a pirate. Francis Drake, the most famous corsair of all time, has acquired a complex popular image, as often happens to great historical personalities. Worse, from his point of view, the negative press comes from Spain: Philip II, whose Invincible Armada Drake decimated, and whose ports and cities from Europe to the West Indies Drake plundered, set a price of 20,000 ducats (approximately 10 million dollars) on his head. Elizabeth I, instead, made him a knight: the Queen certainly did not disdain attractive men who were also criminals (especially if there was booty to share). Some malignant souls even claim she had a son by Drake.

What is unquestionable is that Sir Francis Drake, of modest birth, became one of the richest men of his century. *Forbes* magazine has calculated that in a career lasting forty years on the world's oceans, Drake accumulated wealth equal to (by today's standards) 115 million dollars, nearly all stolen from Spanish

Miniature of 1581, preserved in the National Portrait Gallery in London, with a portrait of the corsair Sir Francis Drake.

galleons or by slave-trading. His patrimony went to his brother Thomas, his grandson Francis, his second wife and the poor of Plymouth, the English port town of which he was once the Mayor. His last will and testament (written and revised between 1585, the year of Drake's second marriage, and 1596, the year of his death) was respected substantially, and apart from the customary disagreements between the lawyers of the beneficiaries, it did not raise particular doubts. Published in England in 1863, Drake's will remains available to any investigator who wants to see the original; it is kept at the National Archives at Kew, in Surrey, England.

So it's no mystery. There is no buried treasure to discover. It's almost a disappointing end for such a celebrated pirate. At least, that's what Oscar Hartzell thought, when he realized that the myth of Drake could use, perhaps, a more romantic conclusion. And so he invented one. And it made him rich, too. If not as rich as his hero, he had enough to live like a prince for fifteen years or so, which, for a soybean farmer from Iowa, wasn't that bad.

From Swindled to Swindler

Oscar Hartzell had nothing to do with either pirates or sailing. Born in 1876 in Madison County, Iowa, Hartzell was a farmer and deputy sheriff. But working the land and studying the law, he felt, were holding him back. His true vocation was as a con man. And what better way for an aspiring con man to realize his potential than to be conned? In 1913, in Des Moines, he met the woman who would change his life: Sudie B. Whiteaker, as she called herself, was a jaunty widow who claimed to know where the legendary treasure of Drake was hidden, and

It is not surprising that the legend of Drake's treasure has dazzled many ingenuous investors: for all his life in fact the English corsair's one purpose, morning to night, was to accumulate wealth. Born in 1540 in Devon, England, Francis Drake first embarked on a mercantile ship when he was thirteen years old. By twenty-two he was a ship captain and was travelling throughout the Atlantic. His hatred for the Spanish began in 1568, when, as the head of a fleet for the Hawkins family of Plymouth (to which he was related), he managed to escape a trap in the Mexican port of Saint Juan de Ulúa. From the 1570s on, he led raids on the Spanish and American coasts, where he captured convoys loaded with gold and silver, plundered entire cities (like Cádiz) and captured Portuguese and Spanish ships between Cape Verde, Panama and Peru.

From 1577 to 1580, aboard the Golden Hind, he completed a circumnavigation of the globe (the first Englishman and second navigator in history to do so): half of the booty he secured on the voyage was for Elizabeth I. It was valued at more than the annual budget of the Crown. England proclaimed him a national hero in 1588, when as vice admiral of the British fleet he contributed to the defeat of the Invincible Armada. But even in this enterprise, his greater interest was in the gold: he risked bringing disorder to his own fleet by undertaking the pursuit and capture of the Spanish galleon Rosario, that transported the wages for the Spanish army. Even in his old age, by then a rich and politically secure man, Drake continued to dedicate himself to naval warfare and pillage. He died of dysentery off the coast of Panama in 1596, while in pursuit of some Spanish ships loaded with treasure.

asked Hartzell to contribute to her project. The farmer considered the proposal, and then went for it, giving Whiteaker 6000 dollars of his mother's savings, hoping for six million in return. Some time passed before he realized he'd been duped. But he'd learned his lesson. In 1921, using the same scheme he'd been taken in by, the hunted became the hunter. He refined the trap.

He contacted various people in Iowa whose surname was Drake, and told them that he was in touch with a direct relative of the corsair (a descendant of the illegitimate son of Elizabeth I), and that they had discovered that the last will and testament of his (and "their") great-great-great-great-great-grandfather had never been honored. The patrimony indeed had been entirely pocketed by the English Crown: revalued with interest over three centuries, their inheritance would now be worth no less than 100 billion dollars. This also included some real estate that the corsair had acquired in his native land, and what was today essentially the entire city of Plymouth, England. The problem now was to find good lawyers and to seek a judgement in a British court. Any person named Drake, Hartzell informed his fellow Iowans, who put a dollar toward this noble cause, was likely to receive at least 500 dollars in the settlement.

A Grassroots Movement

The immediate success of Hartzell's simple plan was miraculous. Thousands of Iowans with the surname Drake began to send him money. Soon the collection was extended to eight other states and even involved people who had different last names. The former farmer and deputy sheriff organized a network of agents in the region to find new contacts and to collect the proceeds: the first were Adna Drake and her husband, W.H. Shepherd, who mortgaged their house in order to put up 5000 dollars, and collected 166,000 dollars from other Drakes – all in good faith. Soon enough, a grassroots movement was underway (it was estimated at between 70,000 and 100,000 people) in support of the enterprise of recovering the Drakes' rightful inheritance from the English. The true talent of Oscar Hartzell was in how he maintained the hopes of his faithful: he organized, in different cities, Drake committees – that had pledged, of course, absolute secrecy, on penalty of expulsion and the loss of inheritance rights – that would periodically convene to read and comment on the news supplied in abundance by their prophet. They sent 2500 dollars a week to Hartzell, who moved to London in 1924 in order "to follow the case more closely." For greater security, all correspondence and money was sent by private courier, to carefully avoid the post service. This was another stroke of genius of the fraudster: for years the police searched the mail for incriminating evidence, turning up nothing. And even when the FBI asked for his extradition, Hartzell had nothing to worry about: he had committed no crimes in England.

Hartzell was absolutely brilliant at encouraging the faith and enthusiasm of his supporters. His power of persuasion was without compare. Even when he got an English girl pregnant, and her furious father confronted him, Hartzell not only managed to calm the man down, he persuaded him to invest 552 pounds in the Drake scheme.

Unconditioned Credit

The game continued undisturbed. Apparently, those who had invested their savings, sometimes mortgaging property or keeping money back from taxes, were content with promises and more and more bombastic announcements, like when Hartzell calculated the total value of the case at 400 billion dollars, an expenditure that would undermine the entire British economy.

Every oscillation of the pound on the market was read as favorable; every week seemed decisive for the outcome of the case. The collapse of Wall Street in 1929, and the Depression, paradoxically, increased the number of applicants to Hartzell's cause. J.M. Keynes, the celebrated English economist, even unknowingly lent a hand in support of Hartzell when he described, in an article, the measures that the English Crown had taken to use Drake's booty to alleviate poverty – a statement read by Hartzell's people as proof of their entitlement. In spite of all the precautions he took, the system began to show some cracks: a few of Hartzell's American agents had used the U.S. Postal Service to communicate. There was an evidence trail, and the FBI found it. In 1933 the prophet of Drake was extradited from London to the United States as an undesirable alien. The trial lasted two years, and naturally Hartzell's lawyers were paid by his aspiring inheritors, who in no way wanted to stop believing in the money that was coming to them. Their hope was so entrenched that even in the year after the sentence (ten years, for fraud) the fund agents collected another half million dollars.

Hartzell wouldn't live to reap his reward. He died in the prison hospital in 1943. But even till the end many of his followers had unshakable confidence in him.

Carlo Pietro Giovanni Guglielmo Tebaldo Ponzi

Carlo Ponzi (United States)

He was not the first, but he was certainly the leader – or one of the forefathers, as some have said – of a school of thought. In finance, he invented Columbus' egg. Or rather, he transformed a brilliant idea – one that seems so obvious in retrospect – into a theorem. The egg had been there for some time. But he picked it up, at the beginning of the twentieth century, perfect, hot, at the best moment. The Ponzi scheme was disarmingly simple; it could be understood even by people who refused to consider arithmetic an everyday science. It just needed someone to try it, to start the mechanism. And that he did, according to legend, with two dollars and fifty cents.

The beginning of Carlo Ponzi's story, told by Ponzi himself to the *New York Times*, seems like a serial novel: he left Naples for America in 1903; and lost the little money he had in card games he played during the crossing in third class. He disembarked in Boston nearly penniless, looked for work, and soon found a job as a dishwasher'. Apart from being homeless, he couldn't be much lower on the social scale. When at last he became a waiter, he shortchanged the customers and was fired. He seemed like a character out of a Victor Hugo novel.

I landed in this country with two dollars and fifty cents in cash and a million dollars in hopes, and those hopes never left me.

The typically proud and mocking expression of Carlo Ponzi, shown in 1920.

Carlo Ponzi was born in Lugo di Romagna on March 3rd, 1882. His father was an official in the Royal Mail – and this, consciously or not, would determine his life – and his mother was from an aristocratic family. The vicissitudes of his father's employment brought the family first to Rome and then to Parma. Carlo was brought up and educated as his family status required: while his parents were content with the public elementary school, for high school he was enrolled in a renowned private institute. He later studied at the prestigious Sapienza University in Rome.

As a university student, Carlo found himself among the sons of very wealthy Italian middle class families, young men who in a night were capable of spending amounts of money in cafés, gambling, and in brothels that he couldn't remotely afford. Carlo lasted two years, and then ended up heavily in debt and with no credit. Soon his only interest was in making money, a lot of money, quickly. It seems his parents were happy to pay for his one-way ticket to America, rather than continue to face impoverishment by their profligate son.

Sign Painter

He landed in Boston on November 15th, 1903. When had money for the ticket, he took a train to Pittsburgh, Pennsylvania, where his cousin Joe DiCarlo and his family ran a general store. A year later, the store failed. In any case, Ponzi was already tired of them and restless.

As Charles – not Carlo – Ponzi, he travelled all over the Northeast. In alphabetical order: New Haven, Connecticut; New York, New York; Patterson, New Jersey; Providence, Rhode Island, and many other places. He tried the most varied jobs. In alphabetical order: dishwasher, insurance agent, sales clerk, sewing machine repairman, steamcleaner, waiter, and workman. On a trip to Jacksonville, Florida, he discovered his talents as a sign painter. Then one night in Providence, he lost everything he'd saved over four years in a game of poker.

No, I never had the slightest experience, but I got away with it [painting signs], satisfied folks, and made a little cash. And all the time I kept dreaming of the time I was going to do big things.

First Act

In 1907, following his losses in Providence, Ponzi arrived in Montreal, Canada, where he found a bank clerk's position at Banca Zarossi. Someone had told him about this bank and its owner, Luigi "Louis" Zarossi, who was concerned, among other things, with the transfer of immigrants' money to their families in Italy. The bank paid 2% on deposits, like all the others, and bought government bonds that yielded 3%. But after making a series of bad real estate investments, the bank had practically no liquidity. To restore it, Zarossi proposed tripling the yield and raising the interest on savings accounts to 6%. To do that, however, the bank would only be able to pay the interest by acquiring, and using, new deposits. Accidentally, more or less, the scheme was already in place. The fact is that in Montreal Charles Ponzi had met – by chance? – a certain Angelo Salvati, an old classmate. Together they promised Zarossi finance from Italy that would save the bank. With their guarantee, Zarossi decided to raise the interest offered.

A short time later, it became obvious that the bank was no longer sending money overseas to immigrants' relatives, and that there was no finance coming the other way, from Italy. Zarossi's bank would fail. His two accomplices advised Zarossi to flee to Mexico with some of what remained in the bank. By then, as they had planned to do, Ponzi and Salvati essentially controlled the bank. But Salvati suggested that it would be better if Ponzi, too, stepped down, because he had been Zarossi's employee. For a while, Ponzi was penniless – apart from a blank check he'd stolen from an important customer of the bank. No problem! Salvati filled out the check, forged the signature, and cashed it at the bank in Charles' name.

One Traitor, Many Friends

The next day, the police turned up at Zarossi's old place, where Ponzi then lived. He was packing his bags. Salvati had cut out his partner, too, and was now the only owner of the bank. Ponzi, on the other hand, was charged, tried, and sentenced to three years in prison. From his cell, he wrote his mother, telling her that he had found a job as a social worker in Canadian prisons.

He was released after twenty months for good behavior. In order to get back into the United States, he needed at least the money for the journey. One of his cellmates had given him a contact: the contact offered him a small sum to get five Italians into the United States illegally. The border police arrested all of them. Ponzi got two years in an Atlanta prison. Inside, he met Charles W. Morse, a banker, who was serving fifteen years for theft. Charles Morse taught Ponzi a lot about swindles, finance, and their syntheses. His most important advice was to always aim high: if you're going to steal, it isn't worth just stealing a little.

A Coupon in the Envelope

In 1918 Ponzi returned to Boston and married Rose Maria Gnecco, whom he met on a streetcar. She was Italian-American, a stenographer, and the daughter of an immigrant fruit and vegetable wholesaler. Ponzi bought the family business and quickly reduced it to bankruptcy.

But for Ponzi, thinking big was an obsession. So he planned another business: writing, exporting, and selling in Europe a vademecum about business, which offered advertising space to local, regional, and international businesses. It was pure marketing, fifty years in advance. All in all, the vademecum did not catch on. It was a flop. But there was a *coup de scène* to the experience that changed the tempo of his life and of this story. In fact, it seems that our hero found what he was looking for in the mail. (A Spanish merchant had responded to one of his queries.) The idea concerned something called an International Reply Coupon. Many immigrants wrote to their families in Europe and wanted to pay for the return-mail, but could not find the stamps of their country of origin. Thus in 1906, the Universal Postal Union introduced the International Reply Coupon. The sender could buy it in any country, and include it with whatever he was sending; the receiver, in turn, could exchange the coupon for a stamp in his country of residence. But the price was very different in poorer countries than in the United States. So Ponzi's idea was to buy the coupons in a poor country, and then sell them in the States. It was a golden opportunity. He earned 10% from coupons he bought in Spain, and more than 200% with coupons from Italy. He began to sell them to his Italian immigrant friends, who were the first to be involved in the business.

Second Act

The scheme, from conception to prison, lasted about a year. It actually operated for eight months, from January to August, 1920. They were unforgettable months: an ex-minor league rogue, uncontrollably ambitious, had in ten months risen to the top, become a name in the great city of Boston.

He promised a 50% return in ninety days: you gave him 1000 dollars, he'd return 1500 in three months. It was too good to be true, too attractive not to try. In the end, 10,000 investors (some say as many as 40,000) paid into Ponzi's plan, generating for the coupon racketeer tens of millions of dollars (around 230 million dollars today).

In February, in a brilliant stroke, Ponzi returned to his first investors their 50% profit after only forty-five days, in half the time agreed. And so it began. The suckers jostled to get in, mortgaging their houses to buy bonds in the Securities Exchange Company that Ponzi had set up at the beginning of the year. The mechanism was elementary, an insult to finance theory: the scheme paid the interest with the new capital invested. In any case, Ponzi did not buy many postal coupons, because he didn't have enough correspondents overseas to purchase them and send them back to him in Boston. Anyway, the Universal Postal Union, precisely to prevent speculation, had, a few months before, changed the long-standing exchange rate that had existed since before the First World War.

So Ponzi did not invest the money entrusted to him in any way. He limited himself to pocketing new investments, and paying his initial investors according to their contracts. In February, he redeemed the first bonds with fabulous interest. Word got around. The increase in returns from his Securities Exchange Company was almost logarithmic: 5000 dollars in February, 30,000 in March, 120,000 in April, 450,000 at the end of May, and millions in June. That same month, he won a legal case against a journalist who had described Ponzi's investment strategy as illegal, and was awarded substantial damages for libel. Meanwhile, by threatening to withdraw all Securities Exchange Company deposits from the Hanover Trust Bank – the local bank he was using to hold

In July of 1920, a man named Joe Daniels filed a claim against Ponzi stating that he had not paid for the furniture in the offices at 27 School Street, and had not repaid a loan Daniels had given him to start the Securities Exchange Company. Daniels asked for nothing less than a million dollars, which was only part of what he was owed from the profits of the scheme. Daniels' action was hopeless, but his accusation would freeze some of Ponzi's bank accounts and draw unwanted attention to his books. In fact, Charles Ponzi had many enemies, especially in the world of banking and finance: the popularity of his Securities Exchange Company had taken money, very quickly, from large, longstanding and established banks and investment firms.

his company's assets – a move that would bankrupt the bank, he forced the bank's partners to sell him most of the stock. Thus Hanover Trust Bank became the operational arm of the scheme.

The Wizard of Finance

Ponzi was five and a half feet tall. He was always ironic, always sure of himself; he wore made-to-measure suits and used oil for hair.

By July, 1920, Ponzi was receiving more than a million dollars a week. Miss Lucy Mell, his chief accountant, extended their activities to various other cities in the Northeast. (In Ponzi's various biographies Mell's age - eighteen years old - is always mentioned, but we cannot understand whether this is an allusion to something).

Ponzi continued to redeem the maturing bonds with 50% interest. At the beginning of the month, the Boston Post dedicated a fairly euphoric front page to him. But immediately afterward, the same paper began to investigate the new financial wizard. Thus the campaign started against the Securities Exchange Company and its tycoon.

A "Gentleman's" Agreement

On July 26th, the *Boston Post* published on its front page an interview with Clarence Barron, a well-known financial expert. "Ponzi does not buy postal coupons," Barron said. In any case, to cover the sums handled by his company, Ponzi would need 160 million coupons. But there were only 27,000 in circulation in the entire world. Some of his first investors showed up at the School Street office: they wanted to withdraw their money. But others continued to believe in Ponzi, and to invest.

Meanwhile, without any legal justification and without authorization from any court, the Boston district attorney began investigating the Securities Exchange Company. Moreover, he proposed a "gentleman's agreement" with Ponzi: to stop the issuing of new bonds until he clarified the situation and addressed public concerns.

Here we find one of the many mysteries of the affair: Why did Ponzi accept the DA's offer, knowing full well that interrupting the issue of bonds could mean the end for him?

He was as cheerful as always, and sure of what he was doing.

A Crowd Waiting for Him

The crowd of worried investors, growing by the day, filled the street where Ponzi's company had its headquarters. He responded by redeeming, over a few days, bonds for 2 million dollars, including interest at 50%. He repaid the starting capital of non-matured bonds. He also offered hot coffee and cookies to thousands of people every morning.

On July 30th, in an interview that appeared in the *New York Times*, Ponzi told his story, and reassured all of his customers.

But on August 2nd, in the *Boston Post*, an article appeared on the front page by a journalist-advertising agent hired by the Securities Exchange Company only a week before (following a suggestion by the director of the Hanover Trust Bank). This time, there was a banner headline over eight columns: *Declares Ponzi is now hopelessly Insolvent*. In the article, Ponzi was described as unbalanced, an idiot, a loser. The author included a long series of calculations, data, and analyses to prove its thesis.

Projects for the Future

It was a terrible, practically fatal blow for Ponzi. For a few more days, he continued to redeem the mature bonds, and even receive requests for new bonds. He remained cheerful.

On August 11th, the *Boston Post* revealed Ponzi's Canadian past, and his convictions.

THE JUDAS CHARACTER

Some time later, it was discovered that the author of the *Boston Post* article was the same person who had informed the Boston district attorney about Ponzi, and that he, an insider, was also the one who had advised Ponzi the financial suicide represented by the interruption of the issuing of new bonds. Another detail that would come to light later was that the journalist was paid about 6000 dollars for the article (about 70,000 dollars today). So that we can render unto Caesar the things that are Caesar's, the Judas in this scene was in reality William H. McMasters, from Franklin, on the outskirts of Boston. At the time he was forty-six years old, blonde, and in archive photos he has the face of a Pinkerton agent. Today when one reads about the entire McMasters affair (his timing, method, the people involved), it appears even more ambiguous. In any case, afterward, no one, except McMasters himself, ever dared to state that he did it out of love for justice.

On August 12th, Ponzi began to talk to the investigators. He was surrendering.

Following his arrest, six banks – including the Hanover Trust Bank, of which he himself was a stockholder – failed. The total loss would be 20 million dollars (about 230 million today). Ten years later, more accurate calculations would reduce the figure to about 4 million.

During his trial, Ponzi talked about his great plans for the future: he wanted to create a new bank and a system of sharing profits between stockholders and account holders; he wanted to launch a subscription campaign to collect 100 million dollars – one million for himself and 99 million to distribute to charity. He wanted to buy old warships and transform them into enormous shopping centers, so as to repay by the sale of every kind of goods the investors who had lost their money in the Securities Exchange Company.

Some people maintain that these projects were the answer to a burning question: Why didn't Ponzi flee with what he had (which was a lot) when it was clear that he was cornered? Ponzi was certainly a swindler, but he was also a foolish visionary. He lost his villa, his two ultra-modern cars, which he had always been proud of, and the money he had in various checking accounts around the Northeast.

Third Act

On November 1st, 1920, Charles Ponzi pleaded guilty and was sentenced to five years in prison. He was released after almost four years but immediately charged by the State of Massachusetts with twenty-two counts of theft and sentenced to another nine years in the slammer. He appealed, and was released on bail. He flew with Rose Maria to Jacksonville, Florida.

September, 1925. Ponzi and his wife presented themselves as Mr. and Mrs. Charles Borelli. The disguise didn't last long: he was too well known. With a Sicilian friend, Calcadonio Alviati, and his wife, he founded the Charpon Land Syndicate (a semi-acronym of Charles Ponzi). They published advertisements in the main national newspapers. They sold empty lots in the Jacksonville area at the very modest price of 10 dollars each. In this case, the mechanism worked as follows: Charpon bought an acre of land for 16 dollars. It then divided the acre into 23 lots, and sold these at 10 dollars each. Ponzi and Alviati could make a profit of 1400%. They also offered bonds for those buyers who wished to participate in the investment. These bonds promised a return of 200% in two months.

In a few weeks the company received thousands of dollars, but it was closed unexpectedly by the authorities, due to bureaucratic technicalities and false company documentation. Indeed, part of the land purchased and subdivided was marshland. Charles Ponzi was sentenced to a year of forced labor. It was April 26th, 1926: Mr. and Mrs. Ponzi had been in Florida for six months. At his sentencing, Ponzi's lawyer appealed. While awaiting the court's decision, he was released on bail. He disappeared, and became a wanted man throughout the United States.

The Flight

In Tampa, on the west coast of Florida, a man named Andrea Luciana, his head shaved and with thick mustache, boarded an Italian cargo ship as a dishwasher and waiter. Around this time, clothing belonging to Ponzi was found on a Jacksonville beach, along with a farewell letter to his wife and his mother. However, the fugitive – now aboard a ship in the Gulf of Mexico – seems to have incautiously revealed his true identity to another seaman. Before sailing toward Europe, the ship docked at New Orleans. There Andrea Luciana/Charles Ponzi was induced to disembark with a trick by a police officer: once on land, he was arrested without a mandate. Ponzi had been, once again, fooled by the law.

Ponzi asked to be expelled from the United States and sent back to Italy. He sent an official request to the President of the United States, Calvin Coolidge. The president ignored it. Ponzi then asked Mussolini for help. He too ignored the swindler.

February, 1927: Ponzi was taken back to Boston to serve the sentence he had fled.

In 1934, when he was released, his wife and two government officials met him at the gate. The latter served him with an expulsion order as persona non grata.

On October 7th, aboard the steamship Vulcania, bound to Italy, journalists, photographers and ordinary people, as in halcyon days, met for a press conference. Little Charles Ponzi greeted President Roosevelt and sent him good wishes. Finally, he announced that his friends had collected enough money to offer him a first class ticket. And this, too, probably means something.

Final Act

No committe welcomed him to Italy when he landed. He wrote an autobiography. Publishers in Italy and in the United States weren't interested. He threatened to publish a memoir, revealing all the dirt on high-society Boston families. But it was just a quip

Rose Maria was to join him in Italy, once he was settled. But he didn't settle, and actually she had no intention of leaving the United States. She filed for a divorce in December of 1936.

When he was down, when he was in trouble, when he was in prison, I stuck to him. When he had millions, when he had a mansion, when he had cars, I stuck with him. And now I feel that I have proved my loyalty through thick and then, and I intend to secure a quiet divorce.

It so happened that Mussolini's personal pilot, Attilio Biseo, was a cousin of one of Ponzi's cousins. In 1939, Biseo became the director of LATI (Linee Aeree Transcontinentali Italiane) and hired Ponzi as an agent in Brazil. In November, the first route was inaugurated: Rome-Seville-Sal-Recife-Rio de Janeiro. Both men moved to Brazil: thus Ponzi crossed the Atlantic once again. In June, 1940, Italy entered the Second World War. Biseo was recalled to Italy. At the end of 1941, the United States entered the war. LATI was shut down. Ponzi stayed in Rio. He continued to write to Rose Maria, who continued not to answer him. He opened first one shop, and then another. Nothing worked. He sold his home. He worked as an interpreter. He was going blind.

At the beginning of 1948, ischemia paralyzed the left half of his body. Thanks to the help of his remaining friends, he found a bed in a public hospital. When his health improved, he told his friends about his plan to for when he would leave. He was cheerful and serene. He died on January 18th, 1949. Shortly before this, in an interview with a New York journalist, he left his finale for his future biographers, little and great:

Even if they never got anything for it, it was cheap at that price. Without malice aforethought I had given them the best show that was ever staged in their territory since the landing of the Pilgrims! It was easily worth fifteen million bucks to watch me put the thing over.

The Match King

Ivar Kreuger (Sweden)

"March 2, 1880 – March 12, 1932. Swedish civil engineer, financier, entrepreneur and industrialist [...] He built a global financial empire founded on the sale of matches." The English Wikipedia page for Ivar Kreuger begins in this way. It's a beginning which leads one to expect a biography full of stories of success, like those of many businessmen who were able to take advantage of the golden years of Wall Street, exploiting the economic boom of the First World War . . . In reality, this was only one side of the coin. The shinier side.

The story of Ivar Kreuger began in 1844, thirty-six years before his birth. It was in 1844, in fact, that Johan Edvard Lundström invented safety matches, matches that lit only if struck against a particular abrasive mixture attached to the edge of the box. They immediately appeared to be safer than traditional matches, and they also lowered the risk of phosphorus contamination during production. This brilliant innovation would be sold throughout the world in only a few years, making fortunes for large and small Swedish producers. One of these was Ernst August Kreuger, who, following the success of his company, was able to enroll his son Ivar at the Royal Institute of Technology in Stockholm.

The Flame of Destiny

At twenty, Kreuger graduated in civil engineering and mechanics, and began to travel the world. He worked in South Africa, Mexico, and in the United States. When he returned to Swe-

---

The entrepreneur and industrialist Ivar Kreuger, center, on the occasion of his visit to Berlin in 1929.

den, he came with not only souvenirs, but professional know-how that was lacking among Swedish engineers of his generation. This enabled him to quickly establish himself: in 1908, together with his cousin Henrik and Paul Toll, another brilliant engineer, he founded Kreuger & Toll, a business specialized in concrete and steel buildings. The company won prestigious contracts, like the construction of the Stockholm Olympic Stadium, which opened in 1912. More or less in the same period, with other partners, Kreuger created a similar company in Germany, Deutsche Kahneisen Gesellschaft mbh (DKG).

Ivar was a confident man who could entertain risk. In contrast to his business rivals, Kreuger's contracts established precise dates for the completion of projects. If he finished early, the clients paid a premium. If, on the contrary, the work took longer, he committed himself to paying out extremely high penalties. These penalties were so high, in fact, that if a project were just two or three days late in completion, Kreuger & Toll could have been driven into bankruptcy. But the clients did not know this.

Ivar was both able and fortunate: winning early gambles with fate, he felt authorized to dream of larger things. So when the opportunity presented itself to buy another company, Kreuger seized it, and soon he discovered that buying companies could be a more profitable game – and more adrenalin-inducing – than designing buildings. He bought various companies, paying not in cash but in bonds from other companies he owned, in their turn bought with bonds of third companies, the value of which was inflated.

When the dark clouds of the First World War appeared on the horizon, and Sweden remained neutral, there were ever more opportunities for both those who had money to invest and those, like Ivar, who didn't have money but knew how to make others believe that he did. He began to buy companies in various sectors: mining, real estate, paper mills. At the top of the pyramid was Kreuger & Toll, which was transformed into a holding company.

Meanwhile, Ivar had begun to run his father's business, which had been in crisis since about 1912. The family's fortune had come from those factories and they could not fail: Kreuger decided to make them the cornerstone of his business.

Swedish Match

He was determined, ambitious, and, by the day, a little more cunning and a little more feared. During the war Kreuger absorbed many of his father's competitors, making use of a tried-and-true method. Once he owned the companies, he transformed them into limited companies and "inflated" their value, using stocks and bonds to purchase new factories of match or raw materials, both in Sweden and abroad. In 1917, after buying the largest Swedish match producer, he merged all the companies into a single group, Svenska Tändsticks (also known as Swedish Match), and succeeded in controlling three quarters of the world market.

By the mid-1920s, Kreuger controlled an empire. And he behaved as a true emperor with all the companies: he re-arranged the balance sheets, moving enormous sums, real and virtual, nonchalantly from one company to another. He understood backwards and forwards the labyrinth of financial transfers and interconnections between his companies. He was the driving force of a system that extended to both sides of the Atlantic:

his companies produced ball bearings, bridges, buildings, film, paper, telephones, gold and other metals, trains and railroad lines. And, of course, matches. Matches, matches, and still more matches.

He used bank loans to buy the very banks that were granting them. He was his own creditor and debtor, and he did not hesitate to create fictitious companies, and make use of nominee to get around laws – especially anti-trust laws that were enforced in the United States – and to speculate on the stock market movements of his companies. He was said to be very, very generous to politicians and civil servants.

By now, Kreuger was one of the most powerful businessmen in the world, to the point of being considered a credible interlocutor by many governments. Those countries with enormous deficits allowed his companies to monopolize the match market in exchange for a commitment to underwrite long-term state bonds, many for enormous sums. From Poland to Hungary, Germany to Estonia, Yugoslavia to Greece, from France to Turkey, the list of countries to which Kreuger lent money (and promised to lend more over the years) is extraordinary: in 1930, his total commitment amounted to more than 380 million dollars, equivalent to more than 10 billion in today's dollars. And in high financial circles it was rumored that he was about to underwrite tens of millions of dollars worth of bonds for Mussolini's Italy.

In practice, after the Great War, he presented himself as the guarantor of the financial stability of half of Europe (and also a piece of Latin America: Ecuador, Guatemala, and Bolivia were his creditors). He launched a sort of prequel to the Marshall Plan, and he managed it himself.

THE MUSSOLINI BONDS

In 1931, Ivar Kreuger was called upon to reassure some creditor banks. He stated that he possessed bonds to the value of tens of millions of dollars issued by the Italian government. (According to different sources, these were between 75 and 150 million dollars). Such holdings should have guaranteed the solidity of Kreuger & Toll. Everyone knew that his holding company had begun negotiations with the Fascist regime to acquire a match monopoly in Italy, but up to that time no one was certain if the negotiations had succeeded: Mussolini did not like publicity in these matters, and Kreuger was famous for his discretion. Nonetheless, under pressure, the financier went so far as to show, in private, a packet of bonds signed by the Italian Finance Minister, Antonio Mosconi, thus reassuring the delegates from the banks. After his death, it emerged that those bonds were counterfeit and the signatures forged. It was a huge scandal and *coup de grâce* to Krueger's reputation. Decades later, however, the writer Lars-Jonas Ångström (the author of the book *Kreuger-Mordet*, which argues that Kreuger was murdered) advanced the hypothesis that those bonds were authentic, and that it was the Fascist regime that led them to be considered false. It was a question of image: Mussolini and his men could not admit that they had trusted a bankrupt lender. But it was also in their interest to make such a claim, because forged bonds, unlike authentic ones, do not need to be redeemed . . .

The Great Depression

Kreuger's success was based above all on the hypervaluation of his companies and on the gamble that his business would continue to go well. Investors from around the world trusted him unconditionally. When Kreuger made agreements with governments, he did not possess the liquidity necessary to honor the underwriting of subsequent tranches of government bonds. When he acquired companies, he paid for them in company bonds of which the real value was much lower than the nominal value. If those possessing bonds of his companies had decided to redeem them, he would have been ruined. To avoid this scenario, it was necessary to make investors believe that his empire was still expanding, so that he could guarantee very high dividends. The boundary between risk and bluff, between creative finance and swindle, can be very narrow, but by now Kreuger had gone well beyond it. And yet nobody suspected anything, nobody dreamed of examining the assets of the Match King, of the tycoon who, starting from practically nothing, had become a multimillionaire. His word was a guarantee. But there weren't many of these. He was a quiet, private man: he gave interviews rarely, and he lived a luxurious life that was shrouded in mystery, which reinforced the myth of the man. In 1929, when he was persuaded to answer questions by a journalist from the Saturday Evening Post, he said that one secret to his success consisted in:

Silence, more silence, and even more silence.

Kreuger's castle began to crumble with the Wall Street crash of 1929, but miraculously it remained standing because most investors continued to believe in him. The problem was that under the castle the ground was shifting. Between 1930 and 1931, the global economic system collapsed, the markets were paralyzed, and, most important, Kreuger & Toll's banks were facing serious crisis: however willing they might be to lend Kreuger more money, they could not do it. Not with the same casualness as before the crash. But Kreuger desperately needed money to honor the commitments already made and pay the high interest rates he had promised to investors.

The collapse was fast and ruinous. In 1931, for the first time, it was rumored that one of his companies would not be able to honor the payment of dividends. A couple of banks began to ask for repayment of loans from the previous years. The tycoon did not give in, and raised the stakes by making an offer for another company, the American IT&T, a giant in telegraphs and telephones, proposing they merge with "his" Ericsson, in order to restore its balance sheet. But for the first time, his counterpart wouldn't follow along, and they asked for an impartial audit. The result was dramatic. His last, dim chance was to ask the Bank of Sweden for help, hoping the Swedish government would decide to save him in order not to put at risk the entire national financial system, which was heavily in debt to him.

On March 11th, 1932, he arrived in Paris, where he had scheduled a meeting with the president of the bank. But on the 12th, he was found dead in his hotel room, shot through the heart. Beside the body was a .357 pistol and a suicide note:

I have made such a mess of things that I believe this to be the most satisfactory solution for everybody concerned.

This is the other side of the coin: Kreuger's castle of financial gambles rested, finally, on nothing. He might have weathered a world war and the Great Depression, but a violent death found him in the end. Ivar Kreuger left the stage forever: suicide, the French authorities declared. It was murder, and a conspiracy, his family would later claim, but there was never a thorough investigation. The only certainty was the tycoon's legacy: a debt of 250 million dollars, and countless investors and creditors left high and dry. Banks, finance companies, and investors all grimly discovered in the end that they were resoundingly mistaken in their valuations. They'd taken for a beacon of economic growth a man who had always been only a match, destined to blow out in the first puff of wind.

The Swindler's Swindle

Arthur Ferguson, or Furguson (France)

Scotsman Arthur Ferguson, or Furguson (1883-1938), elegant and distinguished, probably presented himself to his clients as a man of refined taste, a man worldly and wise. But this we can only guess at, because little is known about the man. Ferguson (or Furguson) was a smooth operator, discreet, keeping out of the limelight until, for instance, he came forward to sell Buckingham Palace, or, on another occasion, the White House, on a ten-year contract.

We first hear of him in 1923, when a tourist from Iowa chanced upon the deal of a lifetime. It was not just a question of money, for the tourist. It was much greater than that: here was a chance to buy a piece of history, to go down in history. Such opportunities did not come around every day. The tourist was in Trafalgar Square, in London, in front of Nelson's Column. He stood in the shadow of the memorial feeling both awe and pride in its presence. It was at that moment that it happened. He was talking to an Englishman, a stranger who had politely stopped to chat, when he realized, suddenly, that he was a lucky man. When people asked him afterward, he could not recall who had started the conversation. Perhaps he, the tourist, had, to ask for information about the monument. But that was not so important.

From the Englishman, the tourist learned everything about the column. He learned, as well, that it – along with the statue of Admiral Nelson that it supported, which was in awful condition – was for sale. Yes, you could see that with the naked eye: the statue had to be restored, like the much of the column. And the British government simply did not have the funds to do this or other equally compelling restoration projects. For that reason, selling it seemed to be the best way forward. For everyone, including Nelson.

Of course, the business was incredibly delicate, and so, for obvious reasons, it was best to keep things quiet.

Just out of curiosity, the tourist asked the price. It would sell to the best offer, the Englishman said. But he expected it to go for about 6000 pounds because the government was in urgent need of funds. However, the column and statue would only be sold to someone who could guarantee its restoration and constant maintenance.

The man stood and looked at the column. It was a picture postcard made of stone, 160 feet tall. It was certainly a surprising way to go down in history for a *parvenu* from Iowa.

And, of course, he would need to take care of the fountain and the base. And take care of the four lions, and the bronze panels with Nelson's victories, made out of the cannons captured from

---

A photo, the best known, attributed to Ferguson (or Furguson); beside it, some of the monuments he sold.

the French, and the leaves engraved in bronze fused from the cannons of the admiral's ship. Everything, the Englishman said.

The lions and the cannons made his cup run over, so to speak. What should he do?

Easy, said the Englishman. He himself, it turned out, was the civil servant entrusted with the sale. But there were some conditions. And they'd already had some offers. You know how it is . . .

The tourist had absolutely no intention of missing out on this great chance. He insisted. He begged. He took out his checkbook, wrote a check, signed it, held it out to the man.

The Englishman did not take it. He once again explained to the man from Iowa just how much work the restoration would require, but also how important it was to keep any transaction a private matter. He recommended a good company for the restoration. And he wanted to be reassured that the American's intentions regarding the monument were sincere, because of its importance to the British people.

Then, after considering the proposal for an appropriate amount of time, the Englishman gently took the check from the tourist's fingers, and in exchange placed in them a signed, stamped receipt. The Englishman and American shook hands and embraced. Then the Englishman slowly went off, turned back a couple times, waving from a distance, and finally disappeared into a crowd looking up at the column.

A Down Payment on Buckingham Palace

During his stay in London, Nelson's Column wasn't the only landmark Ferguson (or Furguson) sold. A few months before, he sold Big Ben for 1000 pounds to another American tourist.

... and if you believe that, I have a bridge to sell you.

(George C. Parker)

Films, songs, even a musical: in the first half of the twentieth century, the sale of the Brooklyn Bridge was legendary. This was because the bridge, along with the Statue of Liberty, was an icon of American life for millions of European emigrants.

Right from the time it was built, Reed C. Waddell, and the brothers Fred and Charley Gondorf, to mention only the best known, repeatedly sold the bridge to immigrant "suckers" or to traveling "suckers" (as they then called tourists), at prices ranging from 200 to 2000 dollars (or 60,000 dollars today).

Once, Fred Gondorf sold half the bridge for two dollars and fifty cents (which was all the sucker had in his pocket). The Gondorfs worked systematically: they had a "Bridge For Sale" sign, which they displayed when they were sure the police were not watching them. Then they convinced the mark of the day by claiming that the owner could make money hand over fist, because of tolls that he could levy, persuading the poor fellow so well that, afterward, the police would have to come by and stop the new "owner" from building toll booths.

Charley Gondorf, alias Charles Douglas, also specialized in horse-race betting scams: his swindle became so common that the police started calling it the "Gondorf game".William McCloundy, from New Jersey, also sold the Brooklyn Bridge a couple times. He was arrested in 1901 and sentenced to thirty months in Sing Sing prison.

George C. Parker (1870-1936) sold the bridge at least ten times. He was a New Yorker who specialized in the sale of monuments and public buildings. He was fond of General Grant's tomb, in Upper Manhattan: he claimed he was the general's grandson. But he also regularly sold the Statue of Liberty, the Metropolitan Museum of Art, and Madison Square Garden.

He used fake offices, always in different locations, and produced mountains of documents to prove his ownership of the property on sale. In 1928, on his third arrest, he was sentenced to life in prison. He died in Sing Sing in 1936.

And then, rather ambitious, and with a Texan, he got 2000 pounds as a down payment on Buckingham Palace.

But all this would surface later on, when Scotland Yard would inform the ingenuous tourist of Trafalgar Square that no one would ever have given him permission to put up scaffolding around Nelson's Column. Furthermore, the monument was never for sale.

At this point, Ferguson (or Furguson) decided to leave for the United States, evidently an excellent market for the articles he traded in. *En passant*, they say he sold the Eiffel Tower as scrap metal. And this is credible, because in those years there actually was talk of dismantling the 1889 World's Fair icon and symbol of *Belle Époque* Paris.

Doing Things in Style

Ferguson (or Furguson) arrived in New York City in 1925. Since he had even crossed the ocean to be there, he decided to do things in style. In Washington he signed a contract with a rancher from out west to rent the White House for 100,000 dollars a year. The first payment was in advance, as always.

Then he returned to Manhattan. One day, he took a ferry out to a little island in the middle of New York Harbor and began to stare at the Statue of Liberty with a mixture of melancholy and resignation, as he had done with Nelson's Column.

This time, the story concerned the expansion of the harbor. The dupe was Australian, though sources disagree on the gender: some say it was a man, others say a woman. The Englishman repeated his performance with meticulous patience, and the Australian, as expected, responded with joyful gullibility.

Or so it seemed. The Australian asked Ferguson (or Furguson) to pose with him (or her) for a souvenir photo. But that's as far as it went. The Australian, suspicious, went to the police and reported the con man.

We Know Very Little, or Rather Almost Nothing

Ferguson (or Furguson) spent five years in prison in New York. When he got out, he moved to Los Angeles where, they say, he successfully continued with his profession until his death. Thus, the shadow of one of the greatest artists of deception dissolved in the golden sun of California.

It is a shame that we know so little about Ferguson (or Furguson). It seems he was an actor. An actor of the second rank, perhaps, without any particular talent, at least in the theater. Apparently, he had a mustache. We have a few photos of him, all very different, so much so that they are like portraits of different people. Similarly, there are few criminal records of the man, in police or prison archives. In fact, before the 1970s, almost nothing was known about the man. And there are suspicious details, like the one in certain accounts that during his theatrical career, in small Scottish theaters, he is supposed to have once played the part of an American who is fooled by a con man. Perhaps this gave him the idea. But it is a piece of the puzzle that fits so perfectly into the rest of the story that it is likely an invention.

One thing is certain: the story of Arthur Ferguson (or Furguson) is a strange one. Sometimes, reading about it, one has the impression that it's a joke, an elaborate trick, a swindle. Even the vowels of his name seem to be up to something.

A Despicable Life

Maundy Gregory (United Kingdom)

Was John Arthur Maundy Gregory (Maundy Gregory to his friends) a man of the theater who became a spy? Or was he predestined – and only predestined – to be an Anglican minister who would become a killer? Or was he a private investigator who became a gossip-column journalist? Or was he a political lobbyist who became a secret agent? Or was he a double-crosser who became a blackmailer? Or was Maundy Gregory simply a killer who'd always wanted to be a con man?

The son of an Anglican minister, Maundy Gregory left Oxford University (and likely an ecclesiastical career) for work in the theater. It was the beginning of the twentieth century.

In 1906 he was accused of swindling the theater company and dismissed. He then set up his own theatrical agency, The Combined Attraction Syndicate Ltd, and, thanks to the financial backing of some well-off people who were friends of an old schoolmate (a pastor who was the director of a boarding school and would later be involved in a famous trial for molesting his pupils), staged a musical. Gregory's company was a miserable failure, and this put an end to his theatrical career. For some years, Gregory directed a private investigation agency that specialized in collecting personal information through restaurants and hotels. In those days there wasn't radio, never mind television . . . Information that wasn't used in investigations ended up in *Mayfair*, a "gossip magazine", in today's parlance, which Gregory himself edited.

Then came the Great War.

Maundy Gregory began to collaborate with the director of MI5, the British counter-intelligence agency responsible for internal security. That brought him into contact with other offices of the intelligence services. One of his tasks was to compile dossiers on the sexual practices of public figures, giving particular attention to any homosexual tendencies. Perhaps not coincidentally,

SECRET RELATIONSHIPS

Gregory's role in MI5, (Military Intelligence, Section 5 – counterespionage) is still not clear even today. By its very nature, links with any intelligence agency are often, by necessity, opaque and indirect. Presently, MI5 refuses to declassify certain reports, even after nearly a century. Therefore, we are still missing some important pieces in the story of Maundy Gregory (born in Southampton, in 1877). What we do have, however, is substantial.

Maundy Gregory, in Bow Street, in London in 1933, during his trial.

at the time Gregory was already an assiduous and frequent visitor of London gay bars and venues. Gossip and blackmail began to play a greater role in his life.

Politics, from the Dirty Side

The first affair involving Maundy Gregory that hit the headlines was the case of Sir Roger Casement, a British diplomat of Irish origins. He was a progressive at the turn of the century, but later became a leader of the Irish struggle for independence. At the beginning of the war, Casement supported the setup of an Irish brigade that would operate in league with Prussia against Great Britain. In 1916 he was arrested for treason. Among his possessions was a diary that clearly revealed homosexual preferences. The diary would play a decisive role in the demolition of his public image, and reduce opposition to his eventual death sentence and execution. Maundy Gregory had already exposed Casement's homosexuality to the secret services. But the suspicion that Gregory himself had placed the diary in Casement's room, prior to his arrest, is harbored by many, and not only the Irish.

In High Society

After the war, Maundy Gregory was welcome in high society drawing rooms, from those of the Liberal Prime Minister, David Lloyd George, to those of the Duke of York (the future King George VI). In 1918, Frederick Guest, who was responsible for the liaison between the coalition government and its parliamentary majority, devised a plan to finance the costs of the government parties by selling honorary titles. Maundy Gregory was the person entrusted to develop the plan, which gave him access to many people among the wealthy and ambitious bourgeoisie.

At first, Maundy Gregory approached only the richest individuals, those he thought most likely to accept the titles he was offering. But words got around and very soon prospective buyers were approaching him. He then developed a third tactic: he would consult the unpublished lists of titles already awarded but awaiting ratification by Parliament, and then attempt to sell these as new. This became – and would remain almost to the end of his life – Maundy Gregory's core business: at the outset, he earned 30,000 pounds a year from service charges alone, and a lot more from the percentages he charged, case by case. He opened an office just off Downing Street; the porter wore the uniform of a government employee.

A Suspect Disappearance

In the same year, a former Labour member of the government returning from the war resumed his campaign against the leading party. Victor Grayson had always been on the margins of the labor movement because of his socialist ideas, fiery oratory and working class support. Gregory was asked to investigate the man. He wrote in his report:

> [...] We believe this man may have friends among the Irish rebels. Whatever it is, Victor Grayson always spells trouble. He can't keep out of it . . . he will either link up with the Sinn Feiners or the Reds. (i.e., the groups that struggle for Ireland's independence).

In some way, Maundy Gregory became acquainted with Grayson. They started spending some time together. In his speeches, Grayson began to denounce the sale of honors by the government as a national scandal. He claimed that Prime Minister David Lloyd George offered knighthoods for 10,000 pounds and baronetcies for 40,000 pounds, and accused him of corruption. He claimed to know the "monocled dandy" that supervised this activity and threatened to identify him publicly. One night in the autumn of 1920, Grayson was beat up by unknown assailants. What was probably an attempt to intimidate him did not have the desired result and his campaign against the title-selling government continued.

On the evening of September 28th, following a telephone call, Grayson left a supper with friends – "Just for a moment," he said. But he never returned. Months later, a person who knew Grayson well claimed to have seen him enter a house by the river Thames on the night he disappeared. But the investigation turned up nothing. Decades later, after many of the participant's in that night's events had passed away, it was discovered that the mysterious house on the Thames belonged to Maundy Gregory. Victor Grayson's body has never been found.

MAUNDY, A MONOCLED DANDY

In his speeches Victor Grayson referred to Gregory as a "monocled dandy," while his biographer, Richard Davenport, described him as "short, big-bellied, balding, ruddy in complexion, monocled and effeminate [...] He could be pompous, mysterious, wary and secretive." He wore a watch inlaid with diamonds, a ring that he said had belonged to Oscar Wilde, and had been given a gold cigarette case as a gift by the Duke of York. In the pocket of his waistcoat, he kept a pink diamond that he boasted had belonged to Catherine the Great of Russia. He radiated confidence and flagrant seduction, distributed gifts, organized suppers and, at times, outrageous parties.

Letter from the Kremlin

In 1922, he moved into a Victorian villa with his "quasi-sister," former-actress Edith Marion Rosse, and her husband. The triangle set tongues wagging. The Bolshevik revolution had occurred in Russia a short time before, and Europe was shocked by the unrestricted war that had broken out between communists and conservatives. Money from Maundy Gregory's sales of honors, which remained a steady source of income, was passed off as funds to support the war against the communists. Four years after Grayson's disappearance, a letter came to light purporting to be from Zinoviev, which asked British communists to initiate protests and riots. The letter, discovered by intelligence services – who vouched for its authenticity – was sent to the Minister of Foreign Affairs. The Prime Minister tried unsuccessfully to keep the letter secret because of imminent elections in Britain. It seems, however, that a civilian employee of MI5 had sent copies of the letter to some newspapers and to the headquarters of the Conservative Party. The Labour members of the government were badly defeated in the elections. In the controversy that raged afterwards, Maundy Gregory was identified as being among the suspected "authors" of the letter.

Poor Edith

A law prohibiting the sale of titles was passed afterwards, but this hardly slowed Maundy Gregory down. Between 1927 and 1931, he bought a club in London and a luxury hotel set in its own grounds in the countryside south of the capital. The latter became the preferred *rendezvous* site for rich London bourgeoisie in pursuit of forbidden weekend pleasures. Both places, the club and the hotel, produced the kind of information that Maundy Gregory had always collected in his dossiers on high profile personalities.

In those years he was not averse to expanding abroad, selling foreign titles, even doing business with the Pope.

Maundy Gregory's turnover in the eight years following the enactment of the law forbidding the sale of titles was said to be around 130 million pounds in today's currency. Despite this, Gregory had financial problems. In particular, in 1932, he had to refund 30,000 pounds for a baronetcy that was paid for but never assigned. For help in the matter, he turned to Edith Marion Rosse, with whom he cohabited (platonically). She rejected his request. However, the problem was soon resolved because within a few months Edith died. It was a sudden passing, although she did have time to scribble her signature beneath her last will and testament, written on a restaurant menu. She left everything to Maundy Gregory. By Gregory's request, the coffin was not sealed (as was customary) and was buried in a shallow grave on the banks of the flood-prone Thames. In this way, when the remains were exhumed, following protests by relatives of Edith, contamination from the waters of the river made it impossible to detect whether there were traces of poison in the body.

A 50 Pounds-Fine

But Edith's money wasn't enough for Maundy Gregory, so he continued as before. However, when he offered a senior officer in the Navy a knighthood for 10,000 pounds the man went immediately to Scotland Yard. The intelligence agencies had been monitoring Maundy Gregory's organizations for years, keeping an eye on his activities.

The Maundy Gregory case was like a bomb in the hands of the Conservative government. First, Gregory denied everything; then he confessed (but only to the present charge, naturally) because the secretary of the Conservative Party promised him a minimal sentence in exchange for his silence: Maundy Gregory had too much dirt on too many people in Parliament to be put on trial as he deserved. The penalty was a 50 pounds fine and two months in prison. The sentence was scandalous.

On his release, from jail he was met by someone who took him to Paris, where he lived out his days on a pension of 2000 pounds a year.

On 28 September, 1941, in a hospital in the occupied Ville Lumière, after being arrested by the Nazis, John Arthur Maundy Gregory died.

Swindler, blackmailer, slanderer, perhaps murderer, perhaps spy: history leaves us a picture of a man who was controversial, ambiguous, clever, equivocal and repugnant. Who knows what truths lie hidden in the documents still protected by the Official Secrets Act.

Count Victor Lustig

Victor Lustig (United States)

He remains the gold standard of con men. He is to the swindle what Summertime is for jazz, Picasso for twentieth-century painting, espresso for coffee. Victor Lustig used and perfected all the techniques still used today, operated in all fields, and he always, regardless of whether he succeeded or failed, practiced his trade with elegance and passion. To this master of the con, we dedicate this volume.

Victor Lustig was born in Hostinné, a small town in Bohemia near the Polish border, on January 4th, 1890. Or maybe not. The name is not recorded in the records of Hostinné's

---

THE TEN COMMANDMENTS OF THE CON ARTIST

We are not certain if these were actually written by Lustig. They are so well adapted to his methods, however, that it is likely that he's the author. In any case, they are attributed to him.

1. Be a patient listener (it is this, not fast talking, that gets a conman his coups).
2. Never look bored.
3. Wait for the other person to reveal any political opinions, then agree with them.
4. Let the other person reveal religious views, then have the same ones.
5. Hint at sex talk, but don't follow it up unless the other fellow shows a strong interest.
6. Never discuss illness, unless some special concern is shown.
7. Never pry into a person's personal circumstances (they'll tell you all eventually).
8. Never boast. Just let your importance be quietly obvious.
9. Never be untidy.
10. Never get drunk.

The sharp gaze and poised elegance of Victor Lustig in a photo from 1937.

communal registrar: nobody with that name was born there on that or any other day. It is probably the case that Victor Lustig was not his real name; or he was born elsewhere. After all, why would someone who is said to have used at least 25 different aliases in his lifetime (some say it's as high as 45) ever reveal his true name and place of birth?

Victor Lustig, the Count, as he used to be called, had two wives. His first, Roberta Noret, he married in 1919. Then they divorced; then they remarried. Then they redivorced. His second wife, Sue Miller, he married in Chicago in 1926 or '27, although at the time he was madly in love with a woman named Ruth Etting, a vaudeville singer with the Ziegfeld Follies. In the same year, Roberta, his ex, married a man named Doug Conner, who we'll hear more about later.

Count Victor Lustig in Six Movements
Episode One: Ocean Liners

In the *Belle Époque* years before the Great War, Lustig traveled back and forth across the Atlantic, between Paris and New York, "earning" all he needed for the trip, including what Roberta required, playing poker.

His residence, if it can be called this, was by then in the United States.

Episode Two: a Small Farm

1922: Lustig (as Robert Duval) bought a small farm from the American Savings Bank, paying 22,000 dollars in Liberty bonds. He changed other bonds for 10,000 dollars. He fled with the packets of bonds and cash. He was caught. When he was brought back to Kansas City, he convinced the bank managers that making the episode public would be bad publicity for them. They give him 1000 dollars for his silence and set him free.

Episode Three: the Eiffel Tower

May, 1925. The Eiffel Tower, built for the Universal Exhibition of 1889, had had better days. It needed extraordinary maintenance, at an extraordinarily cost, and the French government was unwilling to foot the bill. Its demolition was discussed. Lustig called a meeting in a suite at the Hôtel de Crillon, in Place de la Concorde. He invited six major scrap metal industrialists. He introduced himself as the assistant to the general manager of the Ministry of the Post. He had been charged with selling the Eiffel Tower. While he waited for the best offer (plus a separate advance deposit), he demanded of his guests total secrecy about the matter, to avoid protests. In order to convince the chosen victim and his suspicious wife, Lustig's "secretary" (a man named Dan Collins) admitted that the advance payment was his boss's cut, a small "consideration." This rendered everything more credible. With the purchase of the Eiffel Tower the mark – a man from the provinces named André Poisson – expected to break into the serious scrap metal market of the capital. He paid for 7000 tons of scrap metal. Lustig and his accomplice got on the next train for Austria.

Once he realized he had been swindled, Poisson didn't report what happened – to avoid ridicule. Then, after some time, and seeing that Poisson had kept his mouth shut, Lustig and Collins returned to the city and repeated the same scam with another six industrialists. But the mark, this time, didn't follow through in the way they expected him to. Rather, he went to the police. Lustig and the Collins barely escaped. Collins will eventually be caught. Nobody has ever revealed the price set for the Eiffel Tower.

Episode Four: the Romanian Money Box

It was a small mahogany box. A carpenter in New York made it for him. It had slots on two sides for the banknotes. The complicated and noisy motors, inside and outside, were added later. You put a 1000 dollar bill and a sheet of paper into one slot: six hours later, there are two 1000 dollar bills in the other slot. The box, which Lustig called "Romanian," for an exotic touch, was able to duplicate the bills due to the radioactivity of the Radium that it contained. That was it. Apart from the cranks and the levers, which required careful operation, and the long wait, it was as easy as falling off a log. The mark in this case (and the victims should be remembered, too, for their important parts in this comedy of manners) was a man named Herman Loller, a rags to riches multimillionaire. For the Romanian Money Box that, after the demonstration, would never work again, he paid 25,000 dollars (around 300,000 dollars by today's standards). Here, too, Dan Collins lent a hand.

In 1928, Lustig sold a Money Box in Texas – to a sheriff. He is also said to have duped the man with a handful of fake cash. No comment.

Episode Five: Al Capone

Prohibition was at its prime, and the Great Depression lay straight ahead. Lustig insinuated himself into the circle of the most famous gangster of the day, Al Capone. Lustig was fearless.

He convinced the gangster to lend him 50,000 dollars to invest in secure shares. He promised to double the stake in two months. But two months later, Lustig returned the 50,000 dollars to the Chicago boss: the conditions for the operation weren't right. Al Capone appreciated Lustig's integrity and the seriousness with which the man did business. He gave him 5000 dollars, for the disturbance. It is perhaps one of the most brilliant and refined episodes of Lustig's career. This is partly because of the personality involved: nobody would dare, even a century later, call Al Capone a "patsy."

ROBERT TOURBILLON

Robert Arthur Tourbillon, a.k.a. Dan Collins, was one of Victor Lustig's few accomplices. He was in on the sale of the Eiffel Tower and on the money box scheme. Tourbillon started as a lion tamer in a French circus. Locked in a cage, he rode a bicycle around a group of lions. This was his most appreciated number. But for him, it was boring: in 1908, at twenty-three, he emigrated to the United States and began a completely different career. From his initials, he took the nickname "the Rat." He spent several years in various jails, for various crimes, including running prostitutes. Around 1920 he returned to Paris, where he lived for a few years as a *gigolò*, satisfying rich elderly ladies. In 1925, after the second attempt, with Lustig, to sell the Eiffel Tower for scrap metal, he was recognized, identified as a wanted man by U.S. police, arrested, and extradited. It is said that the Atlantic crossing was then, by some twist, transformed into an uninterrupted party at which "Dapper Dan," as the American police called Tourbillon, was the start of the show. Strangely, once back in New York, and on trial, the accusations against Tourbillon were dropped, and he was released. However, he was back in court a few years later, for a 1929 New Jersey swindle, and given two years in the slammer. He was released after sixteen months and, as far as we know, intended to return to France. He was never seen again. If he made it back to Europe, or came to a bad end, is unknown.

One of his great loves (nobody is perfect, indeed) was Billie Mae Scheible, powerful owner of brothels from Oakland to Washington. In 1939, she was sentenced to four years in prison for tax evasion, and the exploitation and trafficking of prostitutes.

When Lustig was in jail, Roberta tried to sell her memoirs in order to recover money even if he did not want her to. One way or another, she was not successul.

His daughter, Betty Jean Lustig, wrote a book with Nancy Garret on the life of her father. *From Paris to Alcatraz*, which she wrote in the 1980s, was published posthumously in 2011. In the book, Betty Lustig writes that Victor had had thousands of lovers (and a long scar on his face from "an irritated" fiancée) but that Roberta had always remained "his wife." (A little "forced romanticism" is unavoidable from a daughter, perhaps, although in the book she uses the name Lustig, not Miller.) She also claims that, in order to protect his wife and daughter, Victor Lustig made them travel continuously, staying in hotels, and always under different names. The family was used to a gilded clandestinity. One morning in the 1940s, Roberta beat cancer with a barbiturate overdose.

The place and date of birth, and other personal information – such as his claim that his father, Ludwig, was once the Mayor of Hostinné – comes from his interrogation preceding his sentencing to Alcatraz. Notes found after his death, among his personal effects, tell instead of a poor upbringing, among peasants. Perhaps he had to learn to steal in order to survive. But elsewhere, it is noted that he attended a university in Paris. In the end, the man's life is full of contradictions, as might be expected from someone who tried to leave as few traces of himself as possible.

Lustig used a dozen passports, spoke five languages fluently, and was wanted by police in forty-five countries.

Only to give an idea: in 1926 alone, with his wife and daughter, Lustig traveled for "work" to New York, Chicago, Detroit, Kansas City, Montreal, Boston, Paris, Cherbourg, Berlin, Munich, Spain and Italy. There were no airplanes or high-speed trains then.

Only steamboats, slow trains, and even slower automobiles. There were few roads and no roadside diners.

According to legend, he started young as a petty thief, a handbag snatcher, a street swindler. He knew all the card tricks.

As a Count, he always wore Chesterfield coats with velvet collars.

The family kept Victor's death hidden for two years. Then a man claiming to be his brother, Emil, began asking for information.

Before arriving at the end: the papers in Lustig's game were so confused – by himself, primarily – that any information about the man, even from the most reliable sources, had to be taken with a grain of salt. As for the rest, the beautiful thing about any movie is that after the first viewing it doesn't matter anymore what is real and what is pretense. At this, too, without question, the Count was a master.

Episode Six: Counterfeiter and Finale

During his long association with Al Capone's gang, Lustig met William Watts, an excellent counterfeiter who could produce banknotes that were practically indistinguishable from those of the Mint. In the early 1930s the two men printed and put into circulation 100 dollar bills to the tune of 100,000 dollars a month. An FBI team caught on to the scam, and followed Lustig and Watts for months before finally arresting them. It was May 10th, 1935, Manhattan. The agent who led the operation was an Italian-American, one Peter A. Rubano. However, the arrest would not bring him much good fortune because he died in Philadelphia four years later. In a photo taken shortly after their arrest, Lustig, surrounded by the federal agents, smiles ironically.

On September 1st, Lustig cut through the bars of his cell, rolled up his bed sheet, tied one end to the bars and lowered himself into the void. Some passers-by saw him, during his descent. He took a handkerchief from his pocket and pretended to be a window cleaner. Then he continued down and, waving goodbye, made a quick exit. His repertoire would not have been complete without one of the most classical jail escapes.

Four weeks later he was caught. There are two accounts of this event: in one, he was caught in Pittsburgh, following a car chase; in the other, he was arrested in a room at the Windermere Hotel, in downtown Chicago. In either case, however, what is clear is that after he broke out of jail, the FBI lost him. They picked him up again due to an unexpected tip. Many years later, Lustig's daughter, Betty Jean, would write that the Judas in the case was none other than Doug Conner, Roberta's second husband. The motive: jealousy.

In order to improve his situation, Lustig revealed the location of a safe deposit box containing 51,000 counterfeit dollars. But the confession didn't help much. In December of 1935, Lustig was sentenced to fifteen years – plus five years, for the escape – in prison. His destination: Alcatraz, the icy rock island penitentiary in the middle of San Francisco Bay.

A warder would recall:

He claimed that he was accused of everything in the category of crime, including the burning of Chicago.

The cold and damp of the prison would kill him. His requests to be transferred and, eventually, to be released for good conduct, were rejected. His demands for medical care, likewise, rejected. He spent over ten years in Alcatraz. On December 30th, 1946, he was taken to the Medical Center at the Springfield Jail, in Missouri. He died there on March 11th, 1947.

We speak of Victor Lustig. But in the records, the prisoner in Alcatraz was a man named Robert V. Miller. Maybe the V stands for Victor. Maybe not.

According to his death certificate, Robert V. Miller was born in Hostinné (with such an un-Czech name); wife: Mrs. Susan Qudback Miller; daughter: Elisabeth Schwartz; cause of death: pneumonia.

With reference to aliases, Betty Jean Lustig wrote in the request for transport of the remains of Victor Lustig from the Springfield hospital to Kansas City: "I, Elisabeth Schwartz, of 7130 Sunset Boulevard, West Hollywood, certify of being daughter of Robert V. Miller . . ."

So the man in jail was Miller. And Lustig?

PS: From what the neighbors remember, 7130 Sunset Boulevard in West Hollywood was always a garage.

The Vermeer
of Deventer

Han van Meegeren (Netherlands)

Han van Meegeren was an unoriginal painter, but he was gifted with extraordinary technique. After a famous critic tore his career to pieces, van Meegeren lived for revenge. He achieved this by forging Vermeers, making copies so perfect that they deceived the expert eyes of the enemy, and even became part of the bloodstained collections of Hermann Göring, number two in Nazi Germany.

Cochineal carmine, charred vine shoots, lapis lazuli powder and phenol, *nigrum optimum*, mercury sulfide, Indian ink, lilac and lavender oil. A hand-built oven, a white jug passed down over three centuries, a dusty map of Europe on the wall, and an old painting, cracked and faded, on his workbench. A feverish light of joy lit his eyes: the alchemist understood that he had finally discovered the perfect formula, the one that would allow him to express his obsession in a concrete form. Henricus Anthonius Han van Meegeren, from Deventer in the Netherlands, born in 1889, was about to bring Jan Vermeer from Delft, who had died in 1675, back to life. He would make him his personal *golem* and would use him to crush, exquisitely, those responsible for the failure of his life.

The Long Wait

Van Meegeren, a painter scorned by the critics and ostracized from the great galleries, in a single move would demonstrate his genius and unveil the incompetence of the so-called experts. All the arrogant people who had derided and offended him, because they were incapable recognizing his true greatness, would be shamed in the eyes of the public. Van Meegeren had discovered how to paint a new Vermeer, or rather the best of the Vermeers: by studying examples by Caravaggio and Rembrandt, he figured out how to create a version of *Supper at Emmaus* that would be superior to every other similar work in terms of composition and evocative power. He would sign the painting with Vermeer's initials, and would then make sure it was seen by Abraham Bredius, the prince of the Dutch "art connoisseurs", the windbag who had torn him to pieces and essentially ended his career.

Van Meegeren painting Christ among the Doctors; *behind him, and out of shot, there are the police and the art critics.*

Then, examining the perfection of *Supper at Emmaus*, old Bredius would proclaim it a masterpiece and attribute the painting to Vermeer. Van Meegeren would then immediately demonstrate that he was the creator of the work, thus destroying his enemy's credibility. Van Meegeren had been around and studied seventeenth-century Dutch painting since his childhood. And he knew that he possessed incredible technical ability, skill recognized by the same men who criticized him for a serious lack of creativity.

To carry out his plan, the artist set up a secret workshop in his house where he could examine all the particularities of Vermeer's painting. He prepared his own paints and varnishes, recovering methods and materials of the artist he intended to bring back to life; he obtained canvases and frames dating from the seventeenth century. He verified the results of countless combinations of binders and pigments to create a painting that aged rapidly, testing various types of heating in the oven to dry the painting artificially. He discovered how to recreate the cracks in the surface of paintings that appear over time, and also how to reproduce the accumulation of dust deposited in those cracks. He even imitated the traces of nineteenth-century restorations which are often present in older paintings. Finally, in order to avoid anachronisms, he decided to paint only objects from the era that he could obtain from reliable antique dealers.

Delayed Revenge

In 1937 everything was ready. Van Meegeren painted his *Supper at Emmaus* and in September instructed a dealer friend to show it to Bredius. The latter fell into the trap, attributing it to Vermeer and taking with him the entire European art establishment.

The "rediscovered masterpiece" was hung in one of the most prestigious museums in the Netherlands and vast numbers of people stood in line to admire it. All at once, a man's voice arose from the crowd: he shouted that the painting was a fake, and that it had not undergone any scientific tests. Those present reacted indignantly; some of them shook their heads when they recognized the disturber as the mediocre painter Han van Meegeren, an artist who, after a promising start, had been reduced to living on sugary portraits produced for the less enlightened middle class. His arrogance was well known, as was his weakness for alcohol.

Rather than reveal himself as the artist, when van Meegeren was confronted and insulted he almost apologized. He explained that he had spoken under the influence of a momentary impression. And, after examining the painting more carefully, he conceded that it was probably authentic. The artist began to consider the benefits of delaying Bredius' humiliation. The painting had been valued at hundreds of thousands of guilders, and the "chance" discovery of another couple of Vermeers could revolutionize his life . . . It could allow him to cultivate to the utmost his extremely expensive passion for women, gambling, and champagne.

For just a moment, his greed for money proved stronger than both the dream of glory and the desire for revenge.

Prison and the Confession

In Europe, the war was in its final days, but for the prisoner trembling in his cell, the battle was just beginning. He desperately lacked his daily dose of morphine, which was essential for him to regain at least a moment of lucidity. And no man should be forced to make the most important decision of his life between one set of withdrawal symptoms and another.

The prisoner's dilemma would challenge even a person in full command of his mental faculties. He could confess the truth, and be freed immediately, but it would mean giving up definitively the wealth he'd accumulated; or he could remain silent, and hope to be released from prison in time to spend his old age on the most beautiful beaches in the world, in the company of beautiful young women.

The public prosecutor was about to change the charges of collaboration with the Nazis and damage to art patrimony to a more dishonorable one, that of high treason. He could be sentenced to life in prison.

His forehead beaded with sweat, on July 12th, 1945, the prisoner Han van Meegeren made his choice. He pleaded not guilty: he stated that he had not impoverished Dutch art patrimony in any way and that he had never collaborated with the enemy. In fact, he explained that he had never sold any painting by Vermeer to the Marshal of the Third Reich, Hermann Göring, and denied the charge. In this connection, he did not deny having sold the high-ranking Nazi *Christ and the Adulteress* signed I.V. Meer, which the Allies had just found. But he explained that the painting was not only a fake, it was also poorly executed, and that he could guarantee with total certainty that the work was not authentic, since he himself was the painter.

On van Meegeren's face, the tension gradually gave way to an angry, sneering, satisfied look: his worry over his financial ruin, which was now inevitable, became less and less important in comparison with his sense of freedom, and above all the satisfaction he felt at the incredulity of his interlocutors. Besides *Christ and the Adulteress*, the prisoner maintained that he had made other paintings attributed to Vermeer by the most illustrious European art historians, and that these had been purchased for enormous sums by museums and collectors. After a minute of silence, he

HERMANN GÖRING AND ART

Hermann Göring, second in command in the Nazi regime, was an insatiable, compulsive art collector. Like a vulture, he was always ready to take advantage of the ruin of Jewish collectors and the weakness of the countries occupied by the Germans to seize minor and major masterpieces, obviously without paying for them or by giving the owners derisory sums. In 2015, a catalogue was published of the works he appropriated: more than 1300 paintings and 250 sculptures, often by great masters such as Botticelli, Rubens, Monet, and van Gogh. At the end of the war, part of the collection was discovered in a secret store in Unterstein, not far from Hitler's "Eagle's Nest". The fake Vermeer painted by van Meegeren was found there. However, many of van Meegeren's other works have been lost.

stated that he had also painted *Supper at Emmaus*. Only one thing marred van Meegeren's pleasure: the awareness that Abraham Bredius would not be forced to pay homage to his talent, and would not have to explain his errors to the press or to the courts. The enemy had cheated him by falling gravely ill before being humiliated.

The Proof

To verify the truth of van Meegeren's statement, the judges decided to force him to paint a fake under police observation; they also appointed a commission of experts with the task of comparing van Meegeren's work with the painting found in Göring's collection and the other Vermeers that the accused maintained that he had copied. To van Meegeren's satisfaction, the composition of the commission caused enormous embarrassment among the critics: almost all Dutch art experts were excluded from the commission because most of these critics had given opinions or judgments on van Meergeren's work, attributing at least one of the works *sub judice* to Vermeer.

The case was a bombshell in the Dutch and international press. To the public, if van Meegeren had really had the guts to palm off a fake to Hitler's deputy, the man charged with high treason would be a hero; and if he had really managed to deceive all the critics, he deserved to be recognized as a master of art. Due to pressure from the media, all the materials requested by van Meegeren for his demonstration were placed at his disposal; the judges also let him to take morphine, without which he would not have been able to concentrate.

With subtle irony, van Meegeren decided to depict the young Jesus debating with the conceited doctors of the Temple. Despite the difficult conditions and the little time available, he completed a painting that was fully compatible with the copies he claimed to have painted. Additionally, chemical analyses carried out on all of the paintings in question showed the constant presence of formaldehyde and phenol. These were substances unknown before the nineteenth century, and van Meegeren had stated, in his confession, that he had used them.

Some members of the commission, reluctant to admit the errors committed in the past, continued to voice reservations about the most important pictures, among which was the famous *Supper at Emmaus*. But very soon they had to capitulate when faced with the other evidence produced by van Meegeren.

Epilogue

On October 29th, 1947, to passionate interest, the trial began. The whole country hoped for acquittal. Van Meegeren's paintings, rediscovered in the stores of the few gallery owners who had deigned to show them, sold like hot cakes. The judges had no doubt: they found him guilty of forgery, in that he had placed on some works the initials of Jan Vermeer. They sentenced him to one year in prison, and forced him to return the money he had illegally earned. The punishment was light because the accused had never declared that the paintings were by Vermeer, but had limited himself to not contradicting the erroneous attributions by the experts. Han van Meegeren barely had time to enjoy his triumph. Worn out by the tension of the last few years and by a life of excess, he died between December 29th and 30th, 1947. He was betrayed by his heart, exactly like Jan Vermeer from Delft three centuries before. With his death, an exceptional forger, perhaps the greatest of his time, was lost. At least, of the forgers we know about, van Meegeren's skill was without compare.

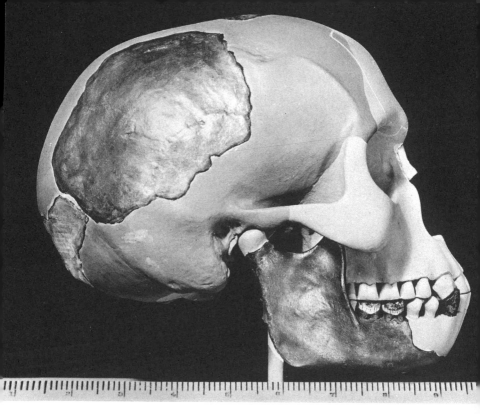

The Piltdown Man

Charles Dawson (United Kingdom)

After the 1859 publication of Charles Darwin's *On the Origin of Species*, archeologists and paleontologists competed to support or oppose the book's revolutionary theory of evolution. Around that time, following the discovery of the remains of prehistoric hominids, scientists and scholars made their first attempts at reconstructing the history of the human species. Similar to the gold rush of the 1840s, scholars after Darwin were driven by "remains fever." Thus, when a self-proclaimed archeologist stated that he had found the missing link between man and monkey, the scientific community was overwhelmed by blind enthusiasm and few were able to maintain a critical attitude toward the discovery.

Charles Dawson, a Sussex lawyer and amateur archeologist, had gained a certain fame in Britain because of some of the artifacts he'd turned up, which ranged from Ancient Roman sculpture to dinosaur fossils. The ground seemed to open willingly beneath his feet, revealing its secrets. While still a young man, his accomplishments were recognized by the British Museum, and he was admitted to the Royal Geological Society of London. But in his vast and diverse collection, he still lacked the one discovery that would make his name go down in history.

Paleoanthropology was still a developing field of research at the time. Only in 1856 were the fossils of Neanderthals first discovered in Germany. They had been buried for thousands of years, and their discovery was followed, in 1891, by the discovery of an older cousin, *Homo erectus*. Everywhere in the world, ambitious paleoanthropologists hoped to make the sensational discovery that would reveal the mystery of our origins: the hunt for the first hominid had started. So, perhaps because of his yearning for further success, perhaps because of his irrepressible British humor, Charles Dawson unveiled his "Piltdown Man," considered today to be the greatest archeological swindle in history.

On December 18th, 1912, the prolific researcher announced, at a meeting of the Royal Geological Society, the sensational finding of remains of what was christened *Eoanthropus dawsoni*. The skeleton was precisely the ancestor everyone was waiting to find, the primate that would prove Man's descent from the monkey

The Wizard of Sussex

What Dawson presented to scientists were fragments of bone which, recomposed with a little flair, constituted a cranium similar to that of modern man, but smaller and with features closer

---

Reconstruction of the cranium of the presumed Piltdown Man, in a photo from 1950.

to those of a monkey. He reported that he had received part of the remains four years before, from a worker in the gravel quarry of Piltdown, in East Sussex. This site became his goldmine: he came across the missing parts of the skull and showed them to Arthur Smith Woodward, the head of the geological department of the British Museum (known today as the Natural History Museum).

In 1912 the two men visited the quarry several times, turning up various remains, among which were stone artifacts, proving the intelligence of the prehistoric hominid. They also "found" remains of animals on the site, doubtless from millions of years before, which confirmed the authenticity of the hominid remains, and moved the dating to an era much more remote than any ventured up to then.

"The Piltdown Man" took shape, and, thanks to the accounts of Dawson, acquired also enviable ability and age. Woodward was enchanted by the discovery, and he became its strongest advocate, arguing how the primate's rise could be placed at a point in time halfway between the chimpanzee and the first *Homo sapiens*.

Dawson died suddenly in 1916, leaving the legacy of his prank to posterity.

Sapiens or non Sapiens

While some immediately suspected that the discovery was questionable, most were ready to welcome enthusiastically a truth that supplied a foundation for their most rooted convictions. So, accompanied by their academic qualifications, they rushed headlong into the trap.

THE EARLIEST ENGLISHMAN

Sir Arthur Smith Woodward was a well-respected paleontologist. He was world famous for his studies on fossilized fish. Many maintain that his involvement in the discovery of the Piltdown Man was done in good faith.

Woodward never recanted. Before his death in 1944, he dedicated himself to writing *The Earliest Englishman*, which offered both a detailed account of the discovery he made with Dawson and conjectures on the life of that ancient ancestor. The book was published posthumously in 1948, five years before the fraud was finally exposed. If Woodward was truly ignorant of everything, then he died holding on to his dream.

In the following years, a series of findings strengthened our knowledge on the origins of modern Man, and described a framework in which the Piltdown Man did not seem to have a place. In fact, it was strange that no subsequently discovered remains, in England and elsewhere in the world, were compatible with the fossils found by Dawson and Woodward. Furthermore, the Piltdown site, after the death of its discoverer, yielded little supporting evidence, and eventually went back to being just a heap of gravel.

The Piltdown Man's life was quite difficult from the very beginning. The hominid's fossils had a lot in common with those of a monkey, which immediately raised suspicions among some scientists. In fact, by recomposing Dawson's fragments more rigorously, critics of *Eoanthropus dawsoni* were able to describe more accurately the brain of the unfortunate primate, thus re-christening the find *Homo piltdownensis*.

Initially, there were only isolated voices claiming that Dawson's fossils could not belong to a single creature. In 1913, David

Waterson, a King's College scholar, dismissed the "remains" as the combination of a man's cranium and the mandible of a monkey, a hypothesis supported two years later by the French scholar Marcelline Boule. The American zoologist Gerrit Smith Miller took these claims a step forward when he attributed the mandible to a prehistoric monkey.

It took forty years of hypotheses and debate to reach a definitive answer to the question of the Piltdown Man. Then, in 1953, using the new technique of radio carbon dating, the Dawson's discovery was unequivocally determined to be a forgery: the head of a hominid was in fact a combination of the mandible of an orangutan (which was about 5000 years old), the skull cap of a Medieval man, and some chimpanzee teeth. One might benevolently suppose that Dawson had involuntarily associated parts of different skeletons found in the same place, but signs of the bones being manipulated, and of substances used to induce artificial aging, proved the artifact was the result of conscious deceit, as was, demonstrably, most of Dawson's collection.

Still, some mystery continues to surround the event: was the Piltdown Man simply a prank that, successful as it was, went too far, or was it a genuine effort at achieving fame and fortune? In any case, Dawson probably died a satisfied man.

Too Good to Be True

The mystery of the Piltdown Man is one that still interests experts today. While the role of Dawson as the brain behind the scheme is now considered almost certain, the question of accomplices remains unanswered. Is it realistic to believe that Woodward, the respected paleontologist, was completely ignorant of the deception? Having analyzed the Piltdown fossils, did he truly believe in their authenticity?

Other more or less well-known figures have been associated with the case: from the Jesuit theologist and paleontogist Teilhard de Chardin, who was accused of obtaining archeological material from Africa, to the writer Sir Arthur Conan Doyle, perhaps only because we like to imagine great minds behind every great deception.

The words of the anthropologist Chris Stringer offer an appropriate warning in this case:

> *If something is too good to be true, then you have to look it as such. [...] The doubts of other scientists were necessary to question everything and to demonstrate that the cranium was not unique: it was simply a forgery.*

A PRANK ENGRAVED IN STONE

On July 23rd, 1938, a commemorative stone was inaugurated at Piltdown, close to the place of the discovery, which preserved for posterity the memory of its place in history. Celebrating the event was the famous paleontologist Arthur Keith, who is still considered a prime suspect in the conception of the scheme. The final words of his inaugural address have proved prophetic: "As long as man is interested in his remote history, [...] the name of Charles Dawson will be remembered."

Nothing could be more true. The monolith still rises proudly over the site, standing as a warning against facile credulity, but at the same time constituting a mocking celebration of human guile.

One Christmas, at Habana Hilton

Prince of Byzantium (Cuba)

Background: the story begins long before the swindle, with a legal case that was followed, not without some sarcasm, by commentary in the daily newspapers and in various genealogy magazines. There were two protagonists. The first was a man from a wealthy Genoese family of ship-owners. He would eventually work as a sales representative for Squibb toothpaste. The second was a man who grew up on the streets in the Sanità neighborhood of Naples. He'd become one of the most successful movie stars of his generation. The name of the first man was Marziano Lavarello; the second was Antonio De Curtis, known on the screen as Totò. The sequel took place in Cuba, in the weeks preceding the flight of Batista and the entry into Havana of Fidel Castro's *barbudos*. The stage: the Habana Hilton, the last great hotel built in Havana with the participation of Cosa Nostra.

The Prince of Byzantium arrived in Havana in December, 1958. Fidel Castro had been leading a guerilla war against the dictator Batista from the mountains in the east of the island. Batista had been abandoned by his American allies. Although diplomats and other agents were accelerating the transition, no one really understood how soon the end would come, or knew what precisely it would bring. It was in this context that, in the first days of December, two Italians arrived in the capital from Milan and set up in two suites of the Habana Hilton. The brand new hotel, opened for only a few weeks, was in the most fashionable quarter of the city.

The two men from Milan arrived at the hotel accompanied by two or three Cubans. In the suites, two other Cubans, one of whom was a very elegant young woman, met them. The Cubans spoke English perfectly. The Italians introduced themselves as the Prince of Byzantium and his personal secretary. They were in Cuba on a diplomatic visit. The only Cuban in the group whose name is on record was their leader, a certain Ricardo Rodríguez, nicknamed Bigote because of his luxuriant mustache. According to his business card, he was a specialist in supplying personalized services to important, wealthy guests. In fact, the Cuban had prepared everything, from the suites to the rumors spreading among tourists. Bigote was especially attentive to visitors from Texas, men who exuded oil money and who were generally more sensitive to proposals favoring their rapid ascent of the social ladder.

Vanity of Vanities

The rumor was that a European Prince was in Havana, and that he was perfectly willing, for a small fee, to grant noble titles, as he had done on previous trips. The chance to become

---

The facade of the Habana Hilton, the luxury Cuban hotel opened on March 19th, 1958.

TWO PRETENDERS TO THE THRONE

It may seem strange, but both Lavarello and Totò claimed to be heirs to the crown of the Byzantine Empire. Yes, the same Byzantine Empire that was overthrown by the Ottoman Turks in 1453. Half a millennium had gone by, but with the title of Emperor of Constantinople one could still make a good impression. How these two made this claim is history, or rather many long histories. What matters for our story is that in the 1950s the claims these men made on the Byzantine Empire crown were recognized by several Italian courts.

So for a time, there were two legitimate heirs to the throne of Constantine the Great. When we consider that the throne was long ago consumed by the worms of history, the situation might not constitute a great problem. But Lavarello's megalomania had no limits, and he challenged Totò many times in court. And although he finally lost the case, paid the legal fees, and was even convicted of calumny, he did not surrender. On November 18th, 1956, in a church in Rome, Lavarello had himself crowned Marziano II, Basileus of Constantinople.

In the process of recognizing these two men as justified claimants to the Byzantine throne, the courts made official corrections to their legal names.

Totò, whose father was unknown, was adopted by an aristocratic family and given the name Antonio Griffo Focas Flavio Angelo Ducas Comneno Porfirogenito Gagliardi De Curtis of Byzantium. For friends and servants, he was Prince De Curtis.

Marziano Lavarello became His Imperial Highness Prince Don Marziano II Lascaris Comneno Flavio Angelo Lavarello Ventimiglia di Turgoville Basileus of Constantinople, Despot of Nicea and Bitinja, Porfirogenito and heir of the Nemanja Paleologo. For his biographers, he was Parrucchino ("Little Wig") I, or even worse. Both were granted by law the *ius honorum*, the right to assign noble titles.

After the coronation, Marziano II returned to live in his palace, a fourth floor apartment on Via Piemonte, in Rome. Occasionally he received guests. Occasionally he granted a title, for payment. But he had ever less money. Lavarello, with his wig, slowly withdrew to the shadows. He died without heirs in 1992.

a count or knight is a great temptation, because vanity is an incurable disease. And so some people began to ask around, wanting to learn more, and the rumor spread. At first, the applicants approached shyly. But then they came in greater and greater numbers.

It is a textbook example: the Prince was reluctant to grant titles. (It's serious business, becoming a count!) But then, facing ever more pressing requests, the Prince gave in. One of the suites became a sort of office where the secretary received the applicants and negotiated prices and formalities with them. Chat at the poolside, or at the casino did the rest. Thus a line formed outside the Prince's Habana Hilton suite: he'd see two or three applicants a day. The title of duke sold for 30,000 dollars. But that was rare. The title of marquis went for 10,000 dollars, and it was more popular.

Clearly, they were professionals. They had all the ingredients: inversion of roles (apparent lack of interest in satisfying the victims' requests), timing, false identity, and money in exchange for a certificate.

Havana, at Christmas

The comings and goings at the Hilton, and the rumors in circulation did not escape the notice of those who controlled the Havana tourist business. They – like Cosa Nostra, or the labor union stockholders of the hotel – expected their cut. Neither did the activity escape the notice of the police or those in the American embassy either.

The Prince and his accomplices had chosen Cuba counting on widespread corruption. They knew that, by sharing part of the loot, they could buy anyone constituting a threat to their plan.

And they chose December because, with Christmas approaching, Havana would be full of generous tourists and their dollars. They hadn't considered the Revolution. However, the Revolution was a lucky stroke for them because all of the officials who in normal times would have wanted to look into their activities were more concerned with saving their necks.

Among other things, according to a delightful touch of hyperrealism in the script, the Prince's secretary seems to have boasted of being Charles Ponzi's son.

What we know for certain is that Marziano Lavarello, at the time, was in his Roman "palace."

Tropical Fog

Che Guevara entered Havana on January 2nd, 1959. Batista had flown to Santo Domingo around midnight of the day before. The tourists abandoned the island *en masse*. The Prince and his secretary left the Hilton a few days later, undisturbed.

In the years to come, all that would turn up of the scheme was the testimony of a few journalists and some Hilton employees. Police documents and reports in the American embassy – assuming that someone noted what was happening at the Hilton at the time – have never appeared.

As one might expect, no victim has ever come forward. (Who would admit to being duped in a scheme like this?) Some victims perhaps never realized what happened, and still boast their honors amid the grazing land and oil wells of Texas. In any case, early in January, 1959, the imperial mission from Byzantium, along with hundreds of thousands of dollars, drifted off into the warm air of the tropical winter.

A Hundred Thousand Times Frank

Frank W. Abagnale jr. (United States)

The genius of Frank W. Abagnale jr. was his ability to insinuate himself into the empty fissures in the gears of banking bureaucracy. An extraordinarily lucky man, Frank used that space to put himself on the border between being and seeming. And as he came to enjoy this unusual mode of existence, he transformed with ease into whatever role he needed in order to face the next challenge. Scriptwriter, producer, and director of himself, he was a con artist auteur, a man with both vision and ethics.

In the dead of night, the corridors of the Smithers Institute of Atlanta echo with a low, urgent voice on the hospital loud-speaker: "Doctor Williams to ER. Doctor Williams to ER". Without running, Dr. Williams takes the stairs, not the elevator. Why do they need him? His responsibilities are almost entirely supervisory, with little to do in accident and emergency. He hopes no one is hemorrhaging. Arriving in the ER he is confronted by three interns grouped around an injured child. The doctor asks why he was called.

"It's probably a fractured shinbone," says Dr. Hollis "X-rays will confirm it."

"What do you think, Dr. Farnsworth?" Williams asks the second intern, who just nods agreement with his colleague.

"Do you agree, Dr. Bice?" he asks the third.

"Simple fracture, Doctor."

"Then you don't need me."

In this 2015 photo, Frank W. Abagnale expresses the same confident and relaxed attitude that he had at twenty.

Fortunately, for nearly a year, nobody had really needed Dr. Frank W. Williams, who had agreed to substitute for the resident supervisor for ten days. But for various reasons, those ten days had turned into months. Frank W. Williams, or rather, Frank W. Abagnale jr., for that was his real name, had moved to Atlanta, Georgia, a short time before, in search of peace and tranquility. He rented an apartment in the luxurious Riverbend Apartment complex, which was very selective in its choice of residents. In order to avoid difficulties, Abagnale had introduced himself as a pediatric doctor, a graduate of Columbia University of New York. Money wasn't a problem; he had enough for a security deposit and the first month's rent. A friendship with a neighboring tenant, a cordial and chatty doctor, led to his being offered a short term of employment as a *locum tenens* in the city hospital. He turned down the offer several times, but then, in order not to arouse suspicion, finally accepted. So he forged a medical degree.

The medical staff, interns, and the nurses were enthusiastic about Abagnale's arrival. They learned a lot under his supervision because he actually let them try things for themselves in their respective fields. Pity that Dr. Williams almost fainted at the sight of the blood, didn't know what "a blue baby" was, nor where to place the stethoscope on a baby's chest. To his credit, however, Abagnale had an insatiable thirst for knowledge, and the impressive ability of being able to memorize anything he heard. He kept a medical handbook locked in a cabinet on the seventh floor of the hospital, his savior every time he came across a word that he didn't know. He spent his evenings watching episodes of *M*A*S*H*, the TV series set in a mobile Army surgical hospital during the Korean War.

The Final Weapon

In reality, what always saved Frank Abagnale was his ability to improvise, to keep calm and make the right decision in the blink of an eye. In an instant he could size up a situation and have a clear idea of what to do next. And his interpretation was always impeccable, better than that of the most consummate Broadway actor.

Moreover, he knew that he must never exceed the unwritten limit, that the slightest excess would be enough to blow his cover completely.

For example, the moment he sensed the danger of continuing the charade, he stopped pretending to be a co-pilot with Pan America World Airways. Without ever having taken a flying lesson, he found himself in possession of a shiny new uniform, a pilot's identity number and card, and, obviously, personal checks to reimburse his expenses.

For Abagnale, his cons were motivated by a specific, ordinary need. He loved women, he was obsessed with them. But to get them, and keep them, he needed money. At fifteen he already looked like a young adult: he was six feet tall, broad-shouldered, with a charming manner.

Girls are not necessarily expensive, he said, but nobody expects to be taken for a hamburger and coke on a date. Lacking financial means, he fell back on the most creative and brilliant part of himself.

A con artist's only weapon is his brain,

he would say in summing up his career. And his brain was a unique, high-precision instrument. It never missed a beat.

The First Scams

In his first attempts to make money with a scam, Abagnale used his father's Mobil credit card, which he could use to pay for minor repairs as well as for gas and oil. To get cash, he needed the owner of a gas station to agree to car repairs that, although they were charged to the card, were never completed. He'd be reimbursed in cash. In a few months he ran up a debt of 3400 dollars. He was proud of himself, and almost driven crazy by the adrenalin rush of pulling off the simple scam. Only when he realized that his father would end up having to pay the debt did he stop doing it, also because his parents were divorcing, and his father found himself in dire financial straits, persecuted by several creditors. When learned about the scam, Abagnale Sr. he forgave his son, but Frank was mortified by what he had done, and looked for a way to set things square. His father was the last individual he swindled.

In 1964 he was sixteen years old and burning to make money. He decided to run away from home and go to New York. There he found work earning 1.50 dollars an hour, a low wage. He pretended to be ten years older than he actually was, doubtless that he looked the part. Soon he got a job earning 2.75 dollars an hour: better – but far from satisfying his ambition.

A scene on the streets of the Big Apple offered the right inspiration: a handsome pilot in uniform walked casually; in his wake his crew, a laughing group of suits and high heels. Beautiful, sleek, elegant, the stewardesses followed the man bewitched, smiling alluringly. "That's what I want to be: a pilot," Frank realized. And, knowing the difference between "being" and "becoming", from that moment on he was already, at least in his imagination, a Pan Am officer. Then it was just a matter of getting others to see him that way too.

How a Swindler Specializes

His experience as a con artist, at that point, was limited to counterfeiting checks. Under assumed names, he had written bad checks for cash many times, seldom being asked if he was actually good for the money. Though by the time that happened, he'd already changed his identity and opened another account. Around that time, early in his career as a swindler, Abagnale began developing his "theory" (as explained in Steven Spielberg's biographical film about the man, *Catch Me If You Can*, 2002). According to Abagnale, there are three fundamental characteristics to every swindler. First of all, the swindler must understand his own personality, must have confidence, and must be careful about his physical appearance, behaving appropriately for each case: gallant with a woman, bold with a bank manager, brazen with a manufacturer. Second, the swindler must be very observant, and have the ability to memorize details. Finally, the swindler must study and learn about every aspect of a planned swindle, creating all of the documents necessary for credibility. The first two characteristics Frank was born with; the third he needed to work hard at. For example, pretending to be a college senior, he interviewed Pan Am managers to get details about work situations, earnings, shifts, permits, and flight procedures. In libraries, he studied all kinds of relevant publications: from magazines he picked up and practiced pilot and airport jargon. He procured the uniform with a phone call, his voice already in character: he is a pilot, the dry-cleaners have lost his uniform and he's on duty in a few hours. No problem: they order a uniform made-to-measure from the nearest supplier. Abagnale also forged an identification card: this was a modified sample ID that had been given to him by a retailer who thought he was a purchasing manager from a new airline. Then everything was ready: the curtain was rising. From that moment, Abagnale traveled coast to coast for free. (In order to get to their next assignment, pilots can ride in the cockpit on the first available flight of any airline.) In addition to free lodging in airport hotels across the country (billed to Pan Am), the wide-ranging mobility let Abagnale cash checks at reception desks or in airport ticket offices without raising suspicion. The checks were counterfeit, but because he'd examined and duplicated every aspect of bank checks – the code string, the perforation, the paper, the stamps – nobody knew the difference. The most important element, however, wasn't in the check itself:

> *Even an off-the-rack dress can pass for the latest fashion if it is worn under a designer coat. [...] What counts is not so much the appearance of genuineness of a check as the appearance of the person presenting it.*

And in his uniform, Abagnale came off as the most credible pilot in uniform in the history of aviation. He received and returned looks of respect and admiration with complete confidence. Maximum courtesy, maximum return. If he caught a bank clerk's eye, she was sure to receive his full and undivided attention. He only hung up the uniform in order to catch his breath, to relax from the constant tension his charades caused him. In 1968 he was twenty years old and had swindled U.S. banks for 2.5 million dollars, changing his identity more than eight times. He had spent as much on custom-made suits, meals in top restaurants, luxury cars and hotels. And he was always in the company of beautiful women. Even when traces and clues of his activities came to light, only much later (when he was already goodness knows where) he risked being caught many times. One time, two deputies arrested him as soon as he got off a plane in Miami. The FBI was on his track and had an open warrant on him. The terms of his employment with Pan Am were raising some questions. But his documents were in order, and under interrogation Frank acted outraged at the accusation, embarrassing the two deputies. The Pan Am New York offices were already closed so the company archives couldn't be checked to see if he was an employee or not. The deputies limited their background check to questioning a stewardess and some of Abagnale's colleagues - names he provided for the investigators. Then, following profuse apologies, he was released.

The Secret of Success is Complete Autonomy

I was an actor, director and independent producer. I knew no professional criminals, I did not seek the advice of professional con men, and I gave criminal haunts a wide berth. The people who helped me in the enterprises were honest, respectable and a little ingenuous: I swindled them because unknowingly they gave me a hand.

In his filmography as a swindler, Abagnale also gave a star performance as a Harvard Law School graduate. Although he forged his law degree, he did manage to pass the bar exam in Louisiana, after which he worked in a prestigious law firm. He was also a sociology teacher for summer courses at Brigham

Young University in Utah; a businessman with a Rolls-Royce; a recruiter (for Pan Am, of course) of aspiring stewardesses, who toured Europe with him for an entire month at the company's expense. In Europe, he perfected his specialization: the father of one of the girls he'd picked up happened to be a printer, and he persuaded the man to print him a book of Pan Am business checks. Now the checks were legion and real. But then, weary of his adventures, Abagnale retired to Montpellier, where he presented himself as a writer and wine connoisseur. He wanted to disappear and enjoy life.

Behind every runaway there is someone in pursuit. Who pursued Abagnale more than all the others was an FBI agent named Sean O'Riley. O'Riley, on the Abagnale's trail for years, traced every step taken by the man he called the "James Bond of the sky."

The French police arrested Abagnale in 1969. He was taken to Perpignan, the worst prison in France, a place where prisoners are treated like animals: locked up "in solitary" in unlit cells, they sleep on the floor, the latrine bucket is hardly ever emptied, there's little food, no washing, no doctor, and no human contact. Abagnale spent six desperate months there before being transferred to Klippan, in Sweden, where he spent another six months. Then he was extradited to the United States, although courts in more than 26 countries – including Italy, Turkey, Spain, Germany, the United Kingdom, Denmark, Cyprus and Lebanon – also sought extradition.

During the transfer to the United States, Abagnale escaped. For him, the airplane was like being at home: he squeezed through a trap door in the toilet, and got out onto the runway soon after the plane touched down. He vanished into the night, to general incredulity. On another occasion, arrested and imprisoned once again, the warders themselves opened the doors of the jail and let him go because he had convinced them that he was a prison inspector in disguise, and that he had infiltrated the prison in order to check its security. He escaped from under the nose of O'Riley many times, but, once caught and finally locked up, his competence and abilities would save his life. He was sentenced to twelve years in prison. After serving five he was eligible for parole, and he began to collaborate with the FBI as an expert on counterfeiting checks and payment instruments – since he could forge checks better than anyone else. He then opened his own agency, Abagnale and Associates, to unmask amateur swindlers and improve the defenses of financial institutions against fraud. Frank Abagnale has changed his life, and now is constantly engaged in the difficult and strangely unfamiliar role of playing himself.

F for Fake

Clifford Irving and Richard Suskind
(United States)

Howard Hughes was an American tycoon, a film producer, director, aviator, and engineer. He was a controversial figure: for a while, he was a national hero, the embodiment of the American Dream; then, overwhelmed by his fall and various scandals, he became a misanthrope, a paranoid, a hypochondriac. In the 1960s, he retired from public life and became a ghost. People were curious about him. The press was desperate for a scoop. The myth grew. What had happened to Hughes? Where was he? Was he sick? Was he dead? In 1972, the billionaire broke his silence. Calling in to a live television program, he wanted to set the record straight.

December, 1970. Nearly ten years had passed since Howard Hughes withdrew from public life. Public and media interest in him had never diminished – although, after years of silence, very little was known about the man. Indeed, a tip-off of his "escape" from his suite in Las Vegas, where he was said to live, on a trip to the Bahamas, drew a lot of attention.

The eccentric billionaire was also of great interest to the American writer Clifford Irving who, at the time, and nearly forty years old, was experiencing writer's block. Suddenly, Irving had an idea. He rung up his friend and colleague Richard Suskind, who was bored to death and heavily in debt.

"What if we wrote Hughes' biography, authorized by Hughes in person?" A guaranteed success, since nothing like it existed. They would propose it to McGraw-Hill, the New York publishing giant, which had already published some of Irving's work. Since they had no actual authorization from Hughes, they would have to commit a small act of literary fraud. But McGraw-Hill would never consent. It would be a fraud that could easily be unveiled by Hughes himself. In any case, Irving and Suskind decided to run the risk, betting that, from his hiding place, Hughes would never find out.

Irving constructed his version of the facts: he had had an exchange of letters with Hughes, in which he had managed to persuade him to edit his autobiography. To prove this, he forged three letters, imitating the magnate's handwriting and signature (which he copied from a real letter that had appeared in a newspaper). McGraw-Hill took the bait. So Irving went ahead with planning the scheme, and pretended to have telephone conversations and personal meetings with the tycoon, during which Hughes established a few conditions: no contact with the outside world and total secrecy of the project. Hughes' well-known paranoia made plausible these otherwise curious demands.

The writer Clifford Irving vents his feelings to journalists after sixteen months in prison.

There were many questionable details about the plan that could have revealed the hoax in an instant. The scheme was ingenious, daring, and maybe a little clumsy. Like many other schemes, after all. But McGraw-Hill trusted its author, fully convinced that they had a best-seller on their hands. Cunning and good luck would do the rest.

An advance of 500,000 dollars – an amount later increased to 750,000 – was to be paid into a Swiss bank account in the name of H. R. Hughes. No one doubted that it belonged to Howard Robard Hughes, the magnate's full name, but the person who opened the account was, in fact, Helga Renate Hughes, which was an alias for Edith Irving, Clifford's wife. She'd used a fake passport.

The mechanism was set in motion, and there was no turning back. The scenario emerging reminded Irving of a comic he had read some years before in *The New Yorker*:

> *A guy falls from the Empire State Building, and on his way past the fiftieth floor someone looks out the window and asks, "How's it going, buddy?" The guy smiles and says, "So far, so good!"*

True and Fake

While they were pretending to meet Howard Hughes, Irving and Suskind used the money and contacts provided by Mc-Graw-Hill to travel all over the United States, in search of material and witnesses. They reconstructed Hughes' childhood, his adolescence, his relationships, his early days in Hollywood, his early successes in business, the legacy of the Tool Company founded by his father, his aerial exploits, the founding of the Hughes Aircraft Company and the acquisition of TWA, Trans World Airlines. Their research turned up every detail of the man's life, right down to the suite in Las Vegas.

They consulted archives and newspaper libraries. They had access to files never made public. By chance, they discovered an unpublished manuscript by Noah Dietrich, the magnate's right-hand man for thirty-two years, which proved invaluable: they obtained unpublished information on business methods, records on conversations the two men had had, even imprecations.

Irving and Suskind ended up knowing him perfectly, but it still was not enough. The autobiography of an extraordinary man like Hughes could not be limited to events that had really happened. The work needed the atmosphere of a novel – it wanted exaggeration, excitement, invention. Thus in "his" autobiography Hughes describes his heroism in the Second World War; he writes of a spiritual journey he took to India; he writes of his friendship with Hemingway, and of his habit of classifying people on a hygiene scale: filthy, dirty, moderately dirty, and fairly clean. The book includes many other surprising revelations. The more incredible and far-fetched they made the stories, Irving and Suskind reasoned, the stronger the desire would be among readers to believe that they were true, and the more difficult it would be to verify them.

Satisfied with the results, they recorded fake interviews, and sent these to the publisher. McGraw-Hill enthusiastically approved of the transcripts. They would serve as the foundation for the book. The life of Howard Hughes began to take shape on the page.

The Sidewalk Began to Loom

At the end of 1971, the book was almost finished. But the house of cards they'd built began to crumble when another authorized biography of Howard Hughes, by Robert P. Eaton, came on the scene. Irving could not cry "fake," to discredit Eaton: to sow any doubt would risk drawing unwanted attention. McGraw-Hill suspected they'd been double crossed by Hughes. Wanting to beat their rival to the punch, the publisher decided to bring out Irving's book sooner than expected. But the ensuing press release created an uproar, and in no time the writer found himself the star of a media circus.

Richard Hannah, Hughes' spokesman, and Chester Davis, his attorney and the Vice President of the Tool Company, immediately denounced Irving's book as a fraud.

However, the letters, the contract signed by Hughes, and as many as two calligraphic examinations confirming their authenticity led McGraw-Hill to feel they were on sure ground. What is more, those who had read excerpts from Irving's book considered the work exceptional, too "real" to be a fabrication.

Although he couldn't stop publication of the book, Hughes did have the last word on the matter. In January, 1972, he phoned the television program 60 Minutes, and broke his long silence:

I don't know Irving. I've never seen him. I've never heard of him before now.

Even if the bodiless voice could be that of an imposter, nobody– not even Irving – doubted that Hughes was really on the other end of the line. And yet it was perfectly consistent with his personality to have dictated an autobiography that he would immediately disown.

By a whisker, the book didn't make it to the shelves. Once the questions started, it was soon discovered that the bank account in Switzerland did not belong to Howard Robard Hughes.

The Weak Link

In reality, a woman had opened it. She was blonde, about thirty-five years old. It did not take long to identify Edith Irving: Helga Renate Hughes' cover was blown, and with it all the rest.

Irving played his last, desperate card: under interrogation, he stated that he had managed the Swiss account through Edith, as requested by Hughes, who did not want anyone in his organization to learn about the autobiography through financial records. But by now then the situation was out of control. Irving's *sangfroid*, his theatrical ability, the trust he enjoyed, were no longer enough. He was defeated, and he confessed to the hoax.

The man in free fall from the top of the skyscraper had crashed to the ground. Nonetheless, his exploit resounds with vast, artistic grandeur.

On June 16th, 1972, Clifford Irving was sentenced to two and a half years in prison. He voluntarily repaid the money he was given by McGraw-Hill. In February of 1974 he was freed on parole. Richard Suskind was sentenced to six months, which was reduced to five for good behavior. Edith Irving served two years in a prison in the United States, and one year in Switzerland.

Howard Hughes died on April 5th, 1976, in a plane crash, on a flight from Acapulco to Houston. His sudden departure from the world's stage left many unresolved doubts. His autobiography, by Irving and Suskind, has never been published (until 2008). Nevertheless, in 1981 a book was published: *The Hoax* by Clifford Irving. At the end of the day, Irving and Suskind had their novel just the same.

A Forger's Career

Tom Keating (United Kingdom)

Thomas Patrick Keating, of a working-class family, wanted to become a rich and famous painter. He had all the technique, but the art world rejected him. So he took his revenge: he flooded British galleries with paintings by famous painters, copies so well executed that not even the painters themselves could have noticed the forgery. For a quarter of a century Keating painted and sold copies of famous Romantic and Impressionist paintings. His work ended up in houses of the wealthy and often in museums. But, as good as he was, he couldn't quiet his vanity, and so in his work he always left a clue to its inauthenticity. The consequences of his act? Nothing less than scandalous.

Samuel Palmer, a Romantic and visionary painter in William Blake's circle, was one of the most loved and most collected British artists of the nineteenth century, desired both by private collectors and museums. The top price at a Christie's auction in

2003 for a small painting was almost 600,000 pounds, while numerous watercolors and etchings of his were valued at between 1000 and 5000 pounds. Around the same time, however, an oil painting by Palmer, a nocturnal scene of extraordinary quality, went on sale at the Brandler Gallery, in Essex, for 35,000 pounds: too little if it was authentic, an enormous sum if it was a forgery.

The gallery owner described the painting as follows:

Created to deceive, this was given to the lawyer that defended him during the Old Bailey Trial. A true Samuel Palmer with ALL the typical Salmer ingredients. Faked, Aged, a true Keating Palmer - better than some of the fakes in the British Museum by Tom.

Besides being an art merchant, John Brandler was also a friend of Tom Keating, who many consider to be one of the best copyists in the world. Brandler said of his friend, "He thought he was at least as good as Rembrandt, Palmer, Renoir, and all the other classic artists put together, and wanted to prove it to the whole world". Keating only lacked one thing, Brandler continued:

He was a meticulous painter. He had all the technical skills, but he was missing the one thing that kept him out of the list of the great painters he copied. He didn't have an original vision.

Perhaps he was not an artist, but he was great, the greatest of forgers.

Twenty-five Years of Honorable Profession

Tom Keating was born in Lewisham, a southeast borough of London, in 1917, into a poor family. He very soon showed he was good with paintbrushes: after the Second World War, he

Tom Keating in front of one of his works.

began to work as a restorer, but to get by he also worked as a house painter. He tried doing paintings, and exhibited them, but he couldn't break through the tough market: it would not be with his paintings that he would finally succeed in making (a lot of) money. "The art market," Keating wrote, "is completely rotten. It is dominated by the fashion of the American avant-garde, with critics and dealers often conniving to line their own pockets at the expense of naive collectors and impoverished artists." Thus, programmatically, he planned to demolish the art system by placing on the market a series of forgeries so well executed that they would deceive even the most discerning critics.

An expert in restoration and art history, he painted in oils using a technique that drew from Titian as much as the Flemish masters: he thus achieved a vast variety of tones and interwoven colors, and achieved unparalleled optical effects. One of the artists he preferred to reproduce was Rembrandt: in order to have the right pigments, he even boiled walnuts for ten hours and filtered them through silk; the color he obtained faded quickly, giving the canvas credibility. He also used old frames from auction houses, inserting in these forgeries of the same painters they had previously contained.

However, Keating was vain, and he considered it important to "personalize" his paintings, to make them appear, on thorough examination, what they actually were: fakes. Thus he prepared the canvases with a coating of glycerin, so that anyone who tried to clean the painting (a common practice in restoration) would ruin the color. Sometimes he wrote sentences in white lead on the blank canvas, sentences that he knew X-ray analysis would easily reveal; often, he introduced anachronisms, or imperfections, into his works. These were his signatures.

Keating stated that he copied no fewer than hundred artists from the Renaissance to the early nineteenth century, and that he had produced, in twenty-five years, about 2000 paintings, which in his Cockney he called "my Sexton Blakes." Many of his works were sold in auction to collectors and museums. His favorite painters, apart from Palmer and Rembrandt, were Thomas Gainsborough, Jean-Honoré Fragonard, François Boucher, William Turner, Vincent van Gogh, John Constable, Edgar Degas, and Amedeo Modigliani. But a detailed list of his forgeries was never released by the forger, to the relief of many investors who preferred, afterward, not to seek an expert opinion on the Impressionist or Romantic painting they had spent a fortune on and which might turn out to be Keating's work.

From the Canvas to the Screen

In 1976, two journalists from *The Times* mentioned Tom Keating's name in connection with an impressive series of watercolors of the "Shoreham period," Palmer's most prolific, which was exhibited in an Old Bond Street gallery. There was a scandal, and perhaps it was just what the forger, who by then was tired and ill, had always wanted. The courts brought to light the painter's career, until then little known, and revealed his extraordinary ability. The young model-lover-manager of Keating, Jane Kelly (she, too, was an excellent painter and restorer, and perhaps, the instigator of the swindle), was given a suspended sentence of eighteen months, after which she emigrated to Canada. Keating's trial was suspended because of his poor health. Years of cigarettes and contact with numerous chemical substances had greatly weakened him. But not enough to prevent him becoming a celebrity. He wrote, with the same journalists who had unmasked him, a bestseller on his life, *The Fake's Progress* (which rhymes with the title of Stravinsky's opera, *The Rake's Progress*), while in the early 1980s he recorded two successful series of documentaries for Channel 4, on historic painting techniques.

Although he was unlucky as a painter, Keating had all the luck of a forger who had confessed but was not redeemed. At a 2004 Christie's auction, over two hundred of Keating's works were sold, earning a notable figure, but the artist couldn't enjoy this belated success: he died of a heart attack in 1984, at sixty-seven. Since then, his fame and the prices of his forgeries have continued to increase, and the ex-house painter Tom Keating, as the gallery owner John Brandler can confirm, has proved to be a safe investment. This happens with all true artists.

THE AMBIGUOUS ART MARKET

Today there are many collectors who purchase, knowingly, Tom Keating's forgeries. "The originals are impossible for the man in the street," one of them declared, "but he gives you ninety per cent of the pleasure for just a small fraction of the price." At the time of the trial, in 1979, no one wanted to know about those works. But after the book, the television programs, and Keating's death, prices have risen astronomically. While in 1984, one could buy a quasi-Cézanne for 1000 pounds, in 1989 Keating's version of Turner's *Fighting Temeraire* sold for more than 27,000 pounds. A recent auction organized by Brad Maurice, the Canadian widower of Jane Kelly, the ex-model and Keating's accomplice, raised no less than 130,000 pounds. The real paradox is that today many fake Keatings (fakes of fakes) are in circulation, a tribute that the forger would have much appreciated. And which confirms his theories on the inherent ambiguity of the art market.

A Ten-Million Dollar Phone Call

Stanley Mark Rifkin
(United States)

It was a question of time. Sometimes you only need a few minutes to do great things; sometimes your life changes in a matter of seconds. Stanley Mark Rifkin knew this very well: he was a computer technician. But not any old engineer – they called him "the wizard of the computer." Computing wasn't his only strength, however. The machines he managed controlled time, sent billions of bits of data whizzing from one part of the world to another. So meticulously did he understand the system protocol and the human procedures that it involved, that he could identify, at any moment, the weakest point in the system. And he could make it submit to his will, to his strategic vision. And in an instant – so suddenly, so unexpectedly – everything happened.

October, 1978. Los Angeles. The sky was cloudless, an azure dome arching over the city. The Security Pacific National Bank building looked like a safe of bronze, glass and concrete in the morning light. Dozens of floors dominated Stanley Rifkin's gaze. And yet it was not the first time he had crossed the threshold of the building. The consultancy he worked for was supervising the creation of a backup system for the bank's data transfer operations.

Rifkin, thirty-two years old, was of medium height, with slightly thinning hair and a youthful, chubby face. He had free access to Floor D of the building, to the room where money transfers took place. As soon as he came in, he politely asked to be updated on the latest operations, and quietly glanced at the sheet where every day the access password, necessary for transactions, was noted. It was an internal code, for the staff, which guaranteed secure operations. It was automatically changed every morning. In order to remember it, employees tended to write it down on a sheet of paper, which made the password quite visible.

After a few hours, Rifkin took the elevator down to the lobby and stepped outside for a breath of fresh air. The sun was already high in the sky. On the Southern California coast in October, it's still plenty warm to swim in the ocean. With the same unassuming elegance of Clark Kent preparing to become Superman, Rifkin slipped into a nearby telephone booth and transformed into Mike Hanson, a bank employee in the foreign exchange department. As Hanson, he called the same office on Floor D that he had just been in, and asked to transfer 10,2 million dollars to the Wozchod Handelsbank in Zürich, where he had opened an account under a false name, via the Irving Trust

Company in New York. Icy beads of sweat ran down his back, and the stuffy air in the phone booth burned his lungs. As he expected, the voice on the line asked him for his extension number, which he naturally gave. Then, as required, it also asked him for the daily security code. His heart was racing heart, he thought he wouldn't be able to speak. But in a perfectly natural tone he said: "4789." "Very good, thank you. Can you give me the transaction number between the two offices?" The question paralyzed him, like an electric shock. He had not foreseen that other numbers and codes were needed! His blood frozen in his veins, and suddenly stiff, like a robot, he said that he would have to call back in a minute, after he checked. He quickly dialed a different extension in the bank and, assuming another identity, obtained the figures needed. Then, as Hanson again, he called back the Floor D office and completed the transaction. He stepped out of the phone booth like a superhero.

Investing in Russian Diamonds

In comparison to sunny Los Angeles, in Geneva it felt like winter. A few days later Rifkin arrived at the Geneva Cointrin International Airport. He had an appointment with Russalmaz, a Soviet government agency which dealt in diamonds. He had been given the contact by Lon Stein, a dealer in precious stones from Los Angeles, to whom he had introduced himself on behalf of the respectable Coast Diamond Distributors. Rifkin already knew how to invest his money.

He made the purchase a few days later: for a little more than 8 million dollars, he was given a case containing 43,200 carats of diamonds. Considering that one carat, the unit of weight for diamonds, is equal to 0.2 grams, Rifkin took with him on an intercontinental flight over 8 kilograms (almost 18 pounds) of diamonds hidden in his belt.

A Quick Ending with Friends

With just one telephone call, Rifkin had managed to pull off the greatest robbery in history. They called him "Jesse James without a pistol": he had the same mythical aura as the nineteenth-century outlaw, but without guns, and without the bloodshed. The bank would not even have noticed the shortfall, if the FBI had not notified them. In any case, once he had completed the arduous part of the heist, disposing of the diamonds turned out to be quite simple for Rifkin. The first jewelry he called, in Beverly Hills, took without question some of his perfectly cut stones. Then he decided to move to Rochester, New York. But there he placed his trust the wrong person. He called up Paul O'Brien, an ex-colleague, to get some advice. He explained the business, but O'Brien, instead of finding him buyers, went straight to the police.

A Scene like in a Sitcom

The police arrested Rifkin in Carlsbad, near San Diego, where he was staying with Daniel Wolfson, a long-time friend. After his exertions and jet lag, the only place he wanted to be was on the windy shore of the Pacific Coast. His arrest, which took place on November 5th, had something theatrical about it. Wolfson, in a burst of pride, tried to prevent the officers from entering his home. With his arms outstretched, as if to embrace the approaching troop, Wolfson formed a human shield. He was easily overwhelmed, however, by the first hint of force. Still, he didn't exactly surrender. Realizing that it was an epoch-making moment, Wolfson seized the tools of his trade (he was a professional photographer) and managed to capture his ex-school mate smiling, almost mockingly, in the moment of his arrest. Minutes later, he called up United Press International and sold the shot he'd just taken for 250 dollars. The FBI was not impressed. They dragged both men off in cuffs, charging Wolfson with harboring a criminal.

The Glass Was Half-Full

Rifkin was detained in the Metropolitan Correctional Center of San Diego and then released on bail. But he'd acquired a taste for telephone transactions: he was arrested again on February

WHAT DOES A BANK DO WITH DIAMONDS?

At the time of his arrest, the police seized a small suitcase from Rifkin containing 12,000 dollars from the Beverly Hills sale, and a blue velvet bag full of diamonds still to be disposed of. At the end of the trial, when at last the Security Pacific National Bank was able to repossess the money it had lost, it had to decide what to do with the diamonds. In the late 1970s, the market value of diamonds was increasing steadily; consultants with the bank suggested that, by keeping the diamonds, they might make a profit of about 5 million dollars on a future sale. For this reason, Security Pacific agreed to maintain ownership, and to pay tax, 10% of the value, as part of the cost of the FBI investigation. Actually, finding a buyer for such a large batch of diamonds turned it to be more difficult than expected: in contrast to gold, silver, and platinum, the valuation of a diamond is subject to many variables. After several failed attempts to sell the diamonds, Security Pacific was forced to use De Beers (a South African diamond mining and trading company) as a mediator, and to agree to the demands of the buyer. The final sale, which took eighteen months to negotiate, was rather disappointing.

13th, 1979. He had used the same scam as before, this time at the expense of the Union Bank of Los Angeles. The epilogue to his adventures was a sentence of eight years in prison.

After his arrest, an old friend of Rifkin, a California State University professor, Gerald Smith, commented in an interview:

The guy is not a bank robber, he's a problem solver. I have a feeling Stan viewed the thing as an incredible problem. He's always five years ahead of anything else going on.

He pulled it off on his first try. After a little while, the cops came for him. Then he got out. He pulled it off again, a second time. And after a little while, in about the same amount of time as before, the cops came for him again. Timing is fundamental in cases like this. But it's not the only fundamental. It's an amateur's mistake, assuming otherwise.

The Great Rock'n'Roll Swindle

Malcolm McLaren (United Kingdom)

People said we couldn't play / They called us foul-mouthed yobs / But the only notes that really count / Are the one that come in wads / They all drowned when the air turned blue / 'Cos we didn't give a toss / Filthy lucre, ain't nothing new / But we all get cash from the chaos.

This is the opening of the song-manifesto by the Sex Pistols, emblematic of their artistic and life philosophy. The title of the song says it all: *The Great Rock'n'Roll Swindle*. The lyrics offer a concise autobiography of the band that was central to the punk movement and generation. The music world, a song like this tells us, for all of its rebels and glamour and tragedy, is little different from any place else: the temptation of an appetizing fraud will stop it in its tracks.

U rban London in the late 1970s: we are in the full flood of a music revolution that will change the face, and a lot more besides, of a generation. It is the outbreak of punk, and Johnny Rotten and the Sex Pistols will be its prophets.

Behind the band that broke all the rules and transformed our understanding of the record industry was a gentleman who wore many hats. Malcolm McLaren (1946-2010), a Londoner, attended art schools and worked in the fashion trade with his wife, the designer Vivienne Westwood. He applied his marketing skills as much to boutiques as to rock bands, to the New York Dolls, for example, an intriguing group for which he was trying to find a new, inventive and audacious look. But his adventures in the Big Apple wouldn't last. In 1976, he launched a large and ambitious project in the newborn field of rock entrepreneurship. Provoking the feelings that govern the decisions of young people, McLaren would distinguish himself as a master of ceremonies, an unscrupulous pioneer, agile and sarcastic in passing himself off as a kind of Robin Hood of the music business. He stole from the rich, to give to the poor (or so he claimed), but above all to give to himself. He talked about his career to the London *Evening Standard*:

> *When I'm old they'll ask me what I did for a living. I will say: I went from office to office picking up checks.*

McLaren, with his business savvy and an innate ability for fraud – as his future clients and the Sex Pistols (his most famous creation) will claim – began to take interest in a small, unknown band, The Strand. Rock was in a state of metamorphosis in 1976, and Malcolm decided on the spur of the moment that The Strand, led by an ill-mannered brat, John Lydon (immedi-

---

Provocative pose and provocative gaze: one of Malcolm McLaren's most typical expressions.

ately dubbed "Johnny Rotten," because of his bad teeth), were the perfect Trojan horse for the take-over war he had in mind.

The image he constructed of the band, after renaming them the Sex Pistols, would be decisive in his attack on the stagecoach of the market, the rules of the musical establishment, a universe of common sense, and quiet, safe and secure middle-class life.

Not One Stone Will Be Left . . .

Punk, say its detractors, is music made by people who can't play, for people who can't listen and don't want to understand. With cynicism and guile, this was a definition McLaren put forward. He came up with a string of *ad hoc* reasons for why the quotations of a group (that substantially doesn't even exist yet) would spread like wildfire, until they became the center of discussion among fans. This interest would find a place in the media, but also in the top positions of sales figures. And here music had nothing to do with it. It was rather, a devilishly conceived plan to take advantage of the energy and the impetuosity of the Sex Pistols, who were game for anything. And for the time being, they were McLaren's perfect ingredient for a magical potion.

Every move he – and consequently they – made was calculated to deliberately raise the levels of scandal, tension, protest, and controversy. All of this energy was then stoked just as much among the trendsetters of the showbusiness world, as it was among the associations that sought to protect families and youth from the contagion of punk. He was burning the candle from both ends.

McLaren struck while the iron was hot. During the Silver Jubilee of Elizabeth II, the Sex Pistols sang a scathing song – irreverently named "God Save the Queen" – from a boat on the Thames (in front of press and TV reporters and photographers); they were consistently met by police and demonstrations outside their concerts and as they stack up denunciations for contemptuous and obscene behavior, they rode the wave of popularity with utter disrespect. Naturally, any question of artistic value was completely ignored. Nobody seemed to care at all for that "marginal" aspect.

McLaren himself wasn't bothered at all. It's business as usual. He was much more lucid and sanguine about drafting and canceling contracts, banking advance payments and forfeits, and steering the band anywhere there was a bonfire to be lit: he was a masterful stage manager who took his show far beyond anything he'd initially hoped for.

The Public Enemy of Conformity

The Sex Pistols, as Lydon explained, were bad boys who did what they had to do in order to enter the confusion of adult life.

SID, BEAUTIFUL AND DAMNED

John Simon Ritchie, alias Sid Vicious, was accused of having stabbed to death his fiancée, Nancy Spungen, in a fight brought on by withdrawal from heroin. He was arrested but got out of jail on bail; he immediately got high, and took a lethal dose. To round up the picture, his mother was involved in the sale of illegal and counterfeit goods. Later, she attempted another fraud: claiming that she kept Sid's ashes in a tin box, she took out an ad in the paper and tried to sell them. But not even her son's poor remains, treated with no respect whatsoever, turned out to be authentic. The memory of the destructive and desolate icon will remain alive and kicking for a long time, largely because of a dark and speculative film, Alex Cox's *Sid and Nancy* (1986). The film, over a hundred minutes long, tells the story of the final weeks in the lives of the two modern anti-heroes.

It was an earthquake for the band, a lightning golden age, and all roads left from McLaren. His limitation, perhaps, was that he never developed their artistic talent: the fuse was short and soon the bluff risked being discovered.

The group also included Sid Vicious, whose only talent was his genuinely terrorizing appearance. He knew nothing about instruments or singing. He was there because of his friend, Johnny Lydon, and his image suited that of a front-man. His was a wretched existence though. His life crushed by heroin, he died dramatically in 1986, just twenty-two years old and on the point of preparing a solo career (some sequences in the film *The Great Rock'n'Roll Swindle*, released in 1980, show what he might have become, as we see him singing two famous cover-versions, "My Way" and "C'mon Everybody" from the repertoires of Frank Sinatra and Eddie Cochran, respectively). It should not have happened under the watchful eye of McLaren, but Sid spoke candidly about him during an interview: "He wanted to be a breath of fresh air. He tried to be artistic and to make an impression to us, but we all laughed. What an idiot. I hate Malcolm."

The Sincerest of Swindles

Vitaliano Fausto's Sex Pistols: *La più sincera delle truffe* ("Sex Pistols: The Sincerest of Swindles"), published in 2013, is one of the many books on the myth and genius of the punk group. Its title speaks by himself: it was, perhaps, a likable, amiable, and romantic swindle, one you would like to believe in. But would we try it again? Partially, yes: the more those indecorous gangsters tried to show us how crude, troublesome, and scornful of quiet living they were, the more their popularity grew.

It was a strange, benevolent spiral for an inexhaustible climber like McLaren, who used the band to make a lot of easy money – money that he kept carefully guarded.

In 1980, at the apex of his career, the double-album *The Great Rock'n'Roll Swindle* was released together with a documentary film made by Julien Temple, which presented – from the point of view of the father-master-manager, McLaren – the band's rise and descent into Hell. The passages that testify to the great rock' n' roll swindle are pitiless and broadcast every sort of unpleasantness to the viewer, to fans and skeptics alike. In a parody of the Ten Commandments, Malcolm/Moses shows how it was possible to create, from nothing, a phenomenon of international proportions like the Sex Pistols.

To balance that biased reconstruction, the same rise and fall of the group would feature in a second film by Temple, viewed

PUNK COMES OF AGE

In many cities in the world, and various ways, 2016 has been celebrated as punk's fortieth birthday: despite resistance by its detractors, punk is a language and a modus operandi that has entered museums, institutions, and the cultural imagination. The writings of punk, its sounds, its graphics, the attitude of the groups that emerged from the barricades in the leading cities of the movement – London, New York, Los Angeles – have left an indelible mark on the style and culture of the present. Punk, cleaned up and refined in the meantime, has been taught and planted in new generations, and today it is easy to find the heritage and traces of that tumultuous season in the field of fashion and design. The stars of the Sex Pistols and their transatlantic lookalikes, the Ramones, have never set; indeed, there appears to be a rising nostalgia for that rough, impolite, distorted, but still not entirely corrupt age.
The flag of punk rock, invincible and epidemic, still flies.

this time through the eyes of Lydon and the survivors: *The Filth and the Fury* (2000) underscored the absolutely central role of McLaren as a fixer.

The scene, and the historical background, remain the same in both films: the fights, aggression, the foul language, noisy Luddism, everything contrary to public decency. They are all the levers of the same slot machine, and they all pay out to McLaren who, having exhausted his project with the Sex Pistols still maintained his position in the business. He continued to produce shows all sorts, and also, under his own name, records (quite interesting and innovative, like those enriched by virtuous duets with Catherine Deneuve and Francoise Hardy, for example).

In the last years of his life, he carried around a quote from one of the filmed interviews. It could serve as his epitaph:

To steal is a thrilling and glorious occupation, above all in the art world.

When Appearances are Deceptive

Melvin Weinberg (United States)

In 1980, the FBI Abscam operation netted a large group of corrupt American politicians and public officials. The person who caught them was a man named Melvin "Mel" Weinberg. A con man for thirty years, Weinberg was arrested only once. While the case had major repercussions for national politics and government institutions, for Weinberg it was both the culmination of and farewell to a long career in white-collar crime.

When Mel Weinberg took the stand as a key witness for the prosecution in a trial about corrupt American politicians, the jury probably gasped in astonishment. The man before them was a skillful swindler, but clearly lacked the charisma one expects from a master of deceit. Thickset, with thinning brown hair on his bald head, the man wore an expensive suit that didn't quite fit. His voice was hoarse, and he had a Bronx accent, and used gangster slang. He was rough and impolite.

Nevertheless, the witness had brought various municipal councilors, publics functionaries and congressmen before the court – no mean achievement for a man who barely finished grade school.

The accused hired the best lawyers to discredit Weinberg and neutralize his testimony. It should not have been such a difficult undertaking: the man's record spoke for itself.

The satisfied face of Melvin Weinberg; in the foreground, the ring with his initials.

Young Swindlers Grow Up

Born in the Bronx in 1924 of a Jewish father and Swiss mother, Mel Weinberg demonstrated his inclination for fraud at an early age. He was six when he started stealing his teacher's gold approval stars, sticking them on his homework to show his marvelous performance in class to his parents.

The strategy worked until he failed. Faced with an incredulous mother, he claimed he was penalized because he was Jewish. But the teacher was Jewish! And so he learned early on a fundamental lesson: always have a credible excuse at hand. He would not be caught off-guard again.

At fifteen, he convinced the rich kids in the neighborhood that he was one of them. He hid his true origins and bragged about his father's flourishing business, financial investments, and his mother's family ties with Swiss bankers. Nobody suspected anything until he had to forego a particularly expensive summer camp, because he couldn't afford it. In the meantime, however, he had developed a taste for luxury that would remain with him for the rest of his life. He made a firm resolution not to want for anything in the future and resolved to "fleece" the rich whenever he could. These are only some of the many indicators that described, in his youth, what type of person Weinberg would become.

Jackets, Socks and Broken Glass

After an adolescence spent learning how to systematically and skillfully steal, Weinberg married a woman named Mary O'Connor, moved to Long Island, and got a job in the family glazing business. But his conduct did not change. He hung out with criminals, did them favors and imitated their manners. He paid to have shop windows broken at night, and employed non-union glaziers. His private life was no model of rectitude, either: he cheated on his wife repeatedly, taking his lovers to a hotel where he paid the police preferential rate (by flashing a police badge stolen by his underworld friends). Women – after money, obviously – were his weakness. And Mary's frequent questions only helped to train his ability to give those fast answers and plausible excuses that would serve him well later on, when he found his true vocation.

Weighed down with gambling debts, he moved with Mary and their three children to Los Angeles in 1952. In his thirties he set up his first true swindles. He began selling defective clothing (jackets without backs and socks without soles, etc.), carefully folded and factory packaged, to suckers convinced they are getting quality articles at giveaway prices. Every morning he was at a different place, to ensnare fresh victims, commuters who in their haste to get to work didn't check the integrity of their purchase.

He returned to New York, divorced his wife, and married one of his lovers, Marie. He continued his upward journey, scaling the tricksters' Mount Olympus. He sold low-grade glass as top quality, leveraging "ethnic pride" – too easy to fail – by fooling Italian-Americans, for example, with fake "Made in Italy" labels. And little by little, he moved up the levels, raising the stakes, until finally, one day, a very profitable and very risky opportunity came his way. It would take a delicate touch.

Upmarket Offices, Suites and Limousines

Introducing himself as an employee of a phantom company by the name of London Investors, Weinberg offered loans to people who couldn't get credit anywhere else. All that was required was an advance deposit. Of course, he warned his customers that he could not guarantee that the banks his company dealt with would grant the loan, and that, regrettably, the deposit was non-refundable in cases of refusal. When, in spite of his warning, the mark decided to proceed, there followed a period of minor confusion, irregularities, and maneuvering. First Weinberg would prevaricate. Then, reluctantly, and with sincere apologies, he would deliver the bad news: no loan. But, given the considerable sum advanced by the aspiring creditor, Weinberg's bank (which didn't exist) was willing to provide a certificate of deposit that could act as a guarantee in seeking a loan from another financial institution. Naturally, the certificate wasn't free.

Weinberg was brilliant, sly, and a great storyteller.

He understood, above all, that the secret of success lies in appearances: he always wore expensive suits, his offices were in elegant buildings, furnished with carefully selected furniture, and the first encounters he had with clients occurred in luxury hotels or in first class suites. He'd send limousines for his clients. And, the cherry on top, he introduced his clients to his partner (and lover), an English woman, Evelyn Knight, who was beautiful, clever, and seductive – even though, according to testimony Weinberg would give later on, the woman had no idea that she was involved in any swindle. She was his unwitting instrument. Weinberg had no problems – psychological, technical, or otherwise – cheating so many people and, despite an occasional setback, among which was a narrow escape from an underworld vendetta, he proceeded for years undaunted with his work. Then, in 1977, a realtor named Lee Schlag smelt something burning and called the FBI. Thus Weinberg's game suffered an unexpected time out.

Serving the FBI

Reported by his last victim, Weinberg was arrested in Pennsylvania, accused of fraud and faced three years in jail. Before his case went to court, however, he struck a deal with the FBI: in exchange for four other arrests, he would serve three years of probation. As sometimes happens, the authorities accept a delinquent into their ranks to take advantage of his special abilities. And so it was that Abscam — an immense sting operation — began in 1978. It was originally aimed at art dealers, but later corrupt politicians and public service functionaries were pulled into the net.

The intended victims were clever, shrewd: only a particularly gifted con man would be able to take them in. John Good, the FBI supervisor who would follow Abscam to the end, was well aware of this: only Weinberg, in his view, could set the scene, lure the victim and spring the trap.

The scene: Agent Tony Amoroso and Mel would pretend to be representatives of two Arab sheiks, Kambir Abdul Rahman and Yassir Habib, owners of Abdul Enterprise Ltd (from which the name of the operation was derived: Ab, from Abdul, and scam, the swindle).

The trap: The sheiks, played by other federal agents – often in an amateurish way, with inappropriate dress and without knowing a word of Arabic – would express interest in bribing politicians in exchange for favors and permits so that they could import stolen works of art and build a colossal casino.

The operation was carried out mainly in hotel rooms and apartments in Florida, New York and New Jersey, where the FBI could hide its television cameras and microphones.

For three years Abscam collected an ever growing number of suspects with Weinberg's assistance. And then, having honored the initial agreement, Weinberg decided to continue his collaboration, but this time on the Bureau's payroll. Among the "victims" who embraced the prospect of so much easy money was – the goose who laid the golden egg – a man named Angelo Errichetti, the mayor of Camden, New Jersey. Before ending up in handcuffs, Errichetti introduced Weinberg to six members of Congress and a Democratic Senator, Harrison A. Williams. Williams would become the first person expelled from the Senate since the Civil War.

MONEY AND MORE MONEY

Following Abscam, Melvin Weinberg was recruited by a private investigation agency founded by a former FBI agent. Later on he accepted an assignment for 65,000 dollars from a Chicago law firm: fashion trade mark owners, including Gucci and Louis Vuitton, wanted to trace and close the businesses that marketed counterfeit bags. The operation was ironically called "Bagscam." Weinberg and his wife Marie separated. He married a woman named Evelyn, but the marriage didn't last. Today, at the age of ninety-one, he lives alone.

In 1981, Robert W. Greene wrote about Weinberg in his book *The Sting Man – Inside Abscam*. In 2013, Weinberg was paid 250,000 dollars for film rights for *American Hustle* (2013), adapted for the screen by Eric Warren Singer and directed by David O. Russell, was critically acclaimed and nominated for many awards. As stated in the opening moments of the film, only some of the events it portrays actually happened. Although the names of the protagonists have even been changed, it is easy, for anyone familiar with the story, to make the connections. "My name is Irving, and bullshit like that," commented Weinberg, laughing, in an interview with *The Telegraph*. In the film Irving Rosenfeld is played by Christian Bale.

The case went to court in 1980. With the Watergate Scandal still very much in recent memory, Abscam further undermined the confidence people had in politicians. At the end of the trial, in spite of the harsh criticism of the methods used by the FBI, the court handed down nineteen sentences. And nobody was able to discredit Weinberg, despite his faults. Indeed, the swindler was able to justify his actions:

An honest man cannot be swindled.

The Son
of Sidney Poitier

David Hampton (United States)

It all began one night in 1983 when David Hampton, then nineteen years old, arrived with a friend at the door of Studio 54, an exclusive New York City club. "You can't come in," the bouncer told them. His friend, without thinking twice, immediately replied: "I'm the son of Gregory Peck." David, tall, lean and black, quickly added: "And I'm the son of Sidney Poitier." To their surprise, the lie worked. They got inside. For David that evening began his career as the "son" of Sidney Poitier and other celebrities, a role that gave him access to high society and put money in his pocket.

D avid Hampton, from Buffalo, New York, was the third son of a lawyer who would eventually disown his son for shame. Family conflict was the norm. "I was an intelligent child, but misunderstood," David said in an interview. "I wanted to enroll in art school, but my father wouldn't let me." So David ran away from home at seventeen. He went to New York City, where he found a world that fascinated him, that stimulated his fervent desire to experiment. He worked at various small jobs until the fateful night he posed as Sidney Poitier Jr. Thus was born the legend of the son of Sidney Poitier, the celebrated American actor who has no male children.

We were swept in like we owned the place. [...] It was sort of a magical moment.

David Hampton in a white bathrobe in his New York home.

High Class Victims

After Studio 54, Hampton's first victim seems to have been the actor and director Gary Sinise. "I was in New York, a guest in Melanie Griffith's apartment. She was living in Manhattan at the time", Sinise said. "She wasn't there when it happened. This boy introduced himself, claiming to be the son of Poitier and a good friend of Melanie. He asked if he could stay over. We spoke till about four in the morning. I let him sleep on the divan. I gave him some money." By passing himself off as the son of a famous "father", David got a place to stay, and money, from Calvin Klein, Melanie Griffith (after she'd come back to the city), and from various celebrities and journalists. The tactic was usually the same: "I'm the son of Sidney Poitier. I just got here, and these guys robbed me down on the street. Think you could lend me some money and a place to stay for the night?" Another version ran like this: "I was late and in a rush – and I got lost getting to the gate – my luggage had already been loaded, see – but then . . . I missed the flight . . . So if you could just lend me a little for the night, my father can settle up with you when he's in the city." On another occasion, in Seattle: "I'm here to interview Bill Gates for *Vogue* magazine. I just arrived. And right out of the taxi, these guys hustle me, take everything! If you could help . . ."

In the Guest Bed with a Friend

In the same year Hampton moved to Connecticut and began to hang out around the Connecticut College. He made friends quickly, telling them that he was engaged in casting for a film, a story based on a Broadway musical comedy. With laid-back *savoir faire*, he was given room and board. At some point, he stole the personal telephone book of Robert Stammers, scion of a New York high-society family. Once back in the city, he called Jay Iselin, the President of WNET television, and his wife Lea. He introduced himself as a friend of their daughter Josie and, following the usual line, he asked for a place to spend the night, and for a little money to tide him over. The Iselins introduced Hampton to the Dean of the journalism program at Columbia University, Osborn Elliott, who agreed to accommodate him in his home for a time. One morning, however, Mrs. Elliott discovered the young man in bed with a friend he had smuggled in during the night. This betrayal of their trust raised the first

HOW HE SAW HIMSELF

David was a handsome young man, tall and slender, fashionable, with a lively mind. From adolescence on, he thought highly of himself. "There was no one who was glamorous or fabulous or outrageously talented like me. I was this fabulous child of fifteen, speaking three languages, and they didn't know how to deal with that", he recalled, without hiding his resentment of his father. To the Elliotts, who reported him and brought him to trial, he showed ingratitude and mockery: "I was the best thing that ever happened to them. I enlivened their lives much the way Norman Mailer livens up Pat Buckley's dinner parties because the other people are boring".
Naturally, once he was released Hampton could not admit to having been in jail. So he said he spent those years in Europe, in Paris, London and Rome, where he maintained himself doing various jobs, from laborer to bartender, to tourist guide. In Paris, in particular, he claimed to have led the life of a king thanks to an old lady who had fallen in love with him. The relation obviously excluded sex: in fact, he made no secret of his homosexuality.

doubts and, after hurried cross checking, David Hampton was reported to the police. On October 18th, 1983, Hampton was arrested, and ordered to compensate his multiple victims with approximately 5000 dollars each. But this money was never returned, so the sentence was changed to four years in prison. He served two and was released on parole in 1986.

Six Degrees of Separation

When the dramatist John Guare came to hear of David Hampton through Osborn Elliott, he was fascinated, and, inspired by his story, wrote *Six Degrees of Separation* (1990). The Off-Broadway play was staged for the first time at Lincoln Center, in New York, and then, a few years later, made into a successful film with Will Smith and Donald Sutherland. Hampton soon became a celebrity. He demanded money from the scriptwriter, since it was his story which had been told, and asked for around 100 million dollars. He did not get the money, naturally, but in compensation he was much in demand in popular media. He gave interviews, all for payment, and appeared on the *TV Files*, a talk show on the Discovery Channel. For his part, Guare claimed he was justified in writing a play on the insecurity, drama and comedy of urban life. After the success of his play and of the film, he reported Hampton several times for making continuous threats.

After his period of fame, David Hampton did not change his ways, though he faced some difficult decisions. He wanted to become an actor, but he spent more time in jail than on the set. He got into trouble over petty crimes. In Seattle again, he introduced himself as Antonio de Montilio, the son of one of the most famous surgeons in the city, who was of Puerto Rican origin. And since his black skin was fair toned, he was easily believed. His last known scam was in 2001. A certain Peter Bedevian later described how David (introducing himself as Dr. de Montilio) invited him to the presentation of a gala show. The tickets ran 1000 dollars apiece. Bedevian had the money and paid in advance. Before the show they stopped at an expensive restaurant, where they ate and drank well, talking and enjoying themselves. But as they were finishing, David got up, with some excuse, and left. Bedevian got stuck with the bill. 400 dollars. However, Bedevian declared:

Honestly? It was one of the best dates that I ever went on.

For Hampton the end was near. He died of AIDS in 2003, in the Beth Israel Hospital of Manhattan. According to a fairly predictable script, after having lived among the stars of New York, he ended his days in complete solitude.

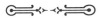

Double Cross

John Gillespie and Hayden Haitana (Australia)

Horse races are cliché in the world of scams. But while most schemes
at the track deal with fixed bets, bribing jockeys, or doping, in the
1980s an Australian story of a race fixed in the light of day made a
sensation. Apparently inspired by ingenuity and optimism, only a
belated revelation suggested that the real scam, which succeeded,
was far more ingenious than anyone at the time realized . . .

The world of betting has always been a breeding ground for
aspiring tricksters. Betting on the favorite is for the weak of
heart, those content with getting a little money from low-risk
investments. The true gambler tries to foresee – in interwoven
probabilities, chance, and technical information – the unexpected result that can win a tidy sum. But sometimes gamblers, the
weak and the great, give a kind word to fate, hoping against
hope that she turns a benevolent eye their way.

When this happens on a racecourse, one witnesses hilarious
scenes of horses that suddenly, inexplicably slow down, or horses
that obstruct each other, getting tangled up, evidently ridden by
jockeys who prefer easy money to sporting fair play. However,
nothing of the sort happened in Australia on the afternoon of August 18th, 1984, at Eagle Farm, the track in Brisbane, Queensland.
The scam started with, in technical terms, a "ring-in": the secret
substitution of one horse for another. The protagonist of the swap
was an Australian thoroughbred, Fine Cotton, an eight-year-old
gelding with a forgettable record. That day, someone decided that
Fine Cotton was going to win. It was a handicap race, in which

John Gillespie with the racehorse Fine Cotton.

the horses carry different weights according to their strength. But Fine Cotton wasn't in the best shape. The odds were 33 to 1. Victory would pay out 33 times the stake.

Great Expectations

In essence, the lower the probability, the higher the winnings in the case of a win: so an unexpected victory for Fine Cotton would be a gold mine. They just needed to make sure that what was highly unlikely would certainly happen. This was the plan for which a gang formed, led by John Gillespie, a former thoroughbred dealer. Also Fine Cotton's trainer, Hayden Haitana, was involved. The first move, Gillespie decided, was to put things in motion in full sight of everyone, replacing the horse with one that was guaranteed to win. The very transparency of the switch, Gillespie was betting, would make the cover work. The estimated prize, should everything fall into place, would be 1.5 million dollars, a figure much higher than the average payout for that kind of race.

Gillespie purchased a horse similar to Fine Cotton, but the animal was injured only a few days before the race. So Gillespie had to find a new animal quickly. He chose Bold Personality, a good, fast horse, used to racing at a higher level. However, while Fine Cotton was dark brown, with white markings on its hind legs, Bold Personality, a year younger, was a bay, a reddish-brown horse, with no markings. To solve this problem, the animal's hair was dyed with hair color, with less than perfect results.

On August 18th, just a few hours before the start of the race, the gang noticed that they had forgotten the hydrogen peroxide they were going to use to bleach the hair on the horse's hind legs. So they used white paint to reproduce Fine Cotton's distinctive markings. Finally, seeing that this rough-and-ready expedient did not prove effective, they bandaged the lower part of Bold Personality's legs.

Meanwhile, in only a few hours the volume of bets on Fine Cotton in all of Australia had risen so much that the odds were shortened to 7 to 2. Despite the suspicions of the racing authorities, the race started without a hitch.

A Podium for Two

Bold Personality, ridden by the novice jockey Gus Philpot – who had no idea that the horse he was riding was not, in fact, Fine Cotton – immediately moved into a front position, and kept pace with the favorite, Harbour Gold. It was a close race that in the end saw Fine Cotton win by half a nose.

The moment the race was over, excited spectators descended on the paddock, shouting that the race had been fixed.

Philpot would later recall:

> *When I got back to the jockeys' room and some of the older blokes were pointing out the window, saying: "You've just ridden a ring-in". And I pulled one of them aside and said "What's a ring-in?"*

The authorities immediately began their inquiry and noticed that rivulets of white paint were trickling down the sweaty legs of the winner. Hayden Haitana took off. He knew immediately that things had taken a turn for the worse. The false Fine Cotton was disqualified, and after an hour Harbour Gold was declared the winner.

The "Fine Cotton Scandal" was not the first of these cases, but it was of particular interest to many because of the important

personalities in the world of Australian horse-race betting who
were involved, men like Bill and Robbie Waterhouse, a father
and son duo from a famous family of bookmakers.

(Perhaps) a Story to Rewrite

In a 2010 interview, John Gillespie told his side of the story. He
claimed to have organized, that August of 1984, a sophisticated
double cross with the complicity of the notorious Sydney criminal and bookmaker Mick Sayers. It was Sayers, Gillespie said,
who had first proposed the ring-in in order to recover losses
from a previous scam.

> *Fine Cotton, the horse, could not win. [...] I don't mind if peo-
> ple think it was a joke or whatever because I walked away with
> 1.8 million dollars.*

According to Gillespie, the ultimate objective of the swindle was not to make Fine Cotton/Bold Personality win, but
to spread the idea that the victory was fixed. He stated that

Hayden, who was in the dark about the double cross, had unknowingly helped the cause.

Hayden had a big mouth, specially when he drank, so we expected he'd talk to people about the ring-in.

In this way, he would have attracted as many bets as possible onto Fine Cotton. Consequently, his odds would have shortened, increasing the odds on Harbour Gold: this was the real objective of the bet. The sham with dyes and bandages was also so maladroit as to evoke a clown's trick'. Thus all the bets on Fine Cotton were annulled, and Gillespie and Sayers – who had bet on Harbour Gold – could claim victory, pocketing more than 12 million dollars.

If we believe this version, new light is shed on the story: the comic efforts of a band of rascals can now be seen as the cunning plan of an expert swindler, a man aware that however things went he would come out the winner. However, Gillespie's claims remained just words, since Sayers, the only person who could have confirmed them, was murdered in 1985. Whether or not Gillespie became as rich as he says he did, we may never know. What's certain, at least, is that his account, twenty-five years after the fact, throws what appeared to be a rather straight forward scam into doubt.

Family Vice

Jean and Nordine Herrina
(France)

The capacity of persuasion, sometimes innate, is certainly a talent that with practice can lead to performances of dizzying conceptual acrobatics. In its simplest form, persuasion operates by aligning the opinions of the persuade with those of the persuader. Any new certainty can be rationally true and broadly acceptable, or founded on the thin base of fiction and falsity. The art of rhetoric is often as much about the acting ability and cleverness of the orator as it is about his language and logic. Take the Prince of Diamonds, for example.

It was a question of persuasion that always concerned Jean and Nordine Herrina. They were uncle and nephew; Jean was an Iraqi of Kurdish origin, born in Rome, and Nordine was Lebancse-Algerian, born in France. They transformed the places they worked into authentic stage-sets, arenas of action where they could demonstrate proof of their gifts: natural actors, they moved with the finesse of magicians. It was a circus they created, a sense of wonder both real and dreamlike, to the point that often their victims, after living as unconscious protagonists in their staging, said it was as if they had been hypnotized.

The scenario: Jean (or Nordine) played a rich Saudi prince or a member of the royal entourage. He wore extremely elegant clothes, had a polished manner, and was always accompanied by a woman who played the silent and variable role of princess, wife or mistress. And as in every staging worthy of the name, there had to be an antagonist: for Jean and Nordine, it was the police. The two con men were among the most wanted men in the world for years.

The Prince of Diamonds

Jean Herrina was a notorious and romantically respected thief. He robbed the most celebrated jewelers in the world. He was an absolute terror to jewelers: a hero to fellow con men and the media, who often related the astonishing vicissitudes of the gentleman-thief with a hint of admiration.

Jean was born in Rome in May, 1956. While still a young man, he married an Italian nomad of French nationality; he became very close to his wife's family, and came to consider himself a gypsy above all else. He resented borders, whether

---

Jean Herrina, an Iraqi of Kurdish origin.

geographical or social. And although he had little education, he was fluent in French, English, Arabic, Italian, and Spanish. He launched his "business" in the early 1980s and immediately concentrated his attention on luxury *maisons*.

In the mid-1990s, Nordine, twenty years younger, took a supporting role to his uncle, beginning a brilliant career. He learned the tricks of the trade, and from his uncle inherited, most importantly, charm, as well as tenacity, and an ability to carefully practice a script until it was flawless. The mechanism was simple, but effective: he pretended to be a wealthy foreign businessman. Accompanied by his chauffeur, he visited the most important jewelries in the world. He was immaculately dressed. At his arm, invariably, was an elegant young woman, in whose name he asked to see the most precious jewels, proposing a five or six-figure purchase. Then, after identifying the objective, and charming the sales clerk, he asked that item he'd chosen to be gift-wrapped; he would then leave the shop with some credible excuse. Before leaving, however, he assured the jeweler that he would return later in the day to settle the bill and collect his purchase. He would generously tip the jeweler as a sign of his good intentions. During the scene, Nordine was affable

THE SCAMMER SCAMMED

Sometimes in life roles are reversed. It happened to Jean once, but only once. A team of African con men managed to get some money from him with the promise of making perfect counterfeits. But the gentleman-thief could not allow such ingenuous and rather clumsy work to go unpunished, so, via some "influential" contacts, he got his money back within a few hours. As always, every step he took was done with the polished elegance and poise that distinguished him.

and discreet, acting naturally, at ease, like an old friend of the jeweler. Obviously, after he left, he would never again cross the threshold of the store, and the scam would be discovered only at the end of the day, when, since the customer had not returned, the jeweler would be forced to unwrap the product and discover that he had gift-wrapped not a precious stone but a spoonful of perfumed air.

A Worthy Disciple

At just twenty years old, Nordine showed he was a worthy heir of his uncle: he began to pull off one robbery after another. He worked in many places: Italy, France, the United States, Belgium, and Switzerland. In a single weekend, he pulled off heists in New York, Florida, and the Bahamas. To give credibility to his multitudinous alter egos, Nordine – or Prince Khalid, alias Al Soud Saad, alias Fimi Wadad — would stay in luxury hotels accompanied by his servants, travel in a chauffeured car or in private jets, wear only designer clothes, and behave appropriately, affably, and persuasively. He also gave generous tips.

Building an alias required perfect identification with the role and an expensive mise en scène. Nordine, like Jean before him, was extraordinary at this. Once he was in character, and in the scene, no one could doubt his identity. In time, he refined his technique, and the number of his victims increased.

The rule was not to leave any clues, never a name, a signature or an address that the police could use to reveal the hidden identity of the prince. He would concentrate a high number of heists within a few days, and then disappear into thin air and wait until the dust had settled. The strategy thus required a mobile,

MILAN: VICTORY AND DEFEAT

In the summer of 2002, the elusive Nordine Herrina managed to get the better of the Italian police in a chase worthy of an action film. Nordine had just gone into a jewelry store in the Via Montenapoleone Fashion District, in Milan. The sales clerks suspected something: Salvini jewelry, nearby, had been robbed in May, and there'd been talk of this elegant secretary of a Saudi princess. They called the police. A car chase ensued, ending at the Piazza della Scala. After firing at the tires, the officers found only one man in the car: Patrick Bernard Grima, Nordine's driver and Marseilles accomplice. Nordine Herrina was caught a few months later, in December. Following a short trial, he was sentenced to three years and four months in prison.

fluent lifestyle: traveling frequently and widely was the best, and only, way to destroy evidence and disappear without a trace.

Too Much Celebrity

Soon, Jean and Nordine Herrina became famous for their sophisticated methods; their mug shots began to cover the walls of jewelers' offices everywhere. So Nordine began to alternate robberies and periods of success with arrests and years in jail. It was a life of ups and downs to which Jean, too, was accustomed. Even in prison, Jean never abandoned the qualities he was known for, and remained affable and elegant. He even revealed his tricks, often transforming interrogations into enchanting reflections on his world, on a life of disguises and illusions. Quite a few investigators became fond of the disarmingly likable and romantic con artist.

Sentenced in 2003 to six years in prison, he escaped by taking advantage of a temporary leave permit. It took two years for police to find him again. He was about to board a flight for Marbella where, in 2002, he pulled off his most sensational heist: he stole a "Golconda," an extremely rare pink diamond worth 3 million euros. Arrested again, Jean Herrina died in Draguignan Prison, on the Côte d'Azur, in 2007. His death was declared suicide, which was inexplicable to anyone who had known him. The final curtain had fallen for Uncle Jean, and it was up to Nordine – who in 2002 boasted robberies amounting to 20 million dollars – to hold high the honor of the family and, who knows, manage to surpass his uncle's exploits.

THEFT ON TRIAL

Jean was proud of his incomparable gifts. He would entertain police officers, men who had made tremendous effort to arrest him, by describing the tricks that enabled him to be one of the cleverest thieves in the world. But he did not limit himself to displaying his ability in the interrogations. In the courtroom, in the middle of a trial, Jean would arrogantly dismiss everyone by stealing the cell phone of the unfortunate judge on duty right under his nose. Although, as any self-respecting gentleman would do, in the end he returned what he'd stolen to its proper owner.

The Secret Agent

Robert Hendy-Freegard
(United Kingdom)

Robert Hendy-Freegard was a semi-literate barman and car-sales-man who passed himself off as an agent of MI5, the British coun-terespionage service, in its struggle against IRA terrorists. Between feigned secrecy, simulated security measures, court appearances and various improbable justifications, Hendy-Freegard successful-ly duped men and women for a decade, taking their money, and making their lives miserable. He was condemned to life in prison in 2005, a sentence reduced to nine years on appeal. "He had a devious charm," Judge Deva Pillay wrote in his verdict

It all began in 1992, when Robert Hendy-Freegard was twenty-one years old and worked as a bartender in the Swan Pub in Newport, England. The place was popular among students from the Harper Adams University, in nearby Edgmond. In a short time Robert became friendly with three of these students: Sarah, Maria, and John. One evening, he revealed to them a secret:

I'm an agent of Her Majesty's intelligence agency, MI5, and I am leading a classified investigation of what we suspect is an IRA cell operating in your university. Obviously, it's a very dangerous one.

The students were excited and proud of being let in on such a secret. But soon, things began to fall apart. Robert alarmed his young friends: if they had been seen with him they were probably in danger. He forced them to go on the run, to cut their links with their families, acquaintances and university colleagues. He exhorted them, in unequivocal terms, to collect all the money they could, because it would be necessary during their time undercover. The three students were quite scared, so they agreed to move with Hendy-Freegard to Sheffield where – while they remained hidden away in a flat for approximately five months – their captor traveled about seducing women and living the good life. During this period, Maria became Hendy-Freegard's lover. In time, she would have two daughters by him.

The Lie Must Be Big

His philosophy was simple and entirely mad:

Lies have to be big to be convincing.

He said so to the police who interrogated him in 2002. Hendy-Freegard applied this principle without hesitation. When the

---

Robert Hendy-Freegard poses for the police camera.

mother of his daughters began to rebel, he beat her without mercy and advised her not to tell anybody, "for security reasons." And when another of his victims threatened to go to the police, he claimed that the police force had been infiltrated by IRA agents. If they spoke to the wrong person, it would be the end. Robert's imagination seemed limitless. One time, he imposed a fidelity test on a man he had already cleaned out of 300,000 pounds and engaged in his phantom intelligence service. He asked him to go to a certain store to buy a can-opener and to deliver it, in secret, to a bartender in a certain pub. Called to testify in court, the poor man admitted he had delivered the can-opener to the bartender as directed, who had watched him first with surprise, then with baffled amusement.

Women Are Better

Robert Hendy-Freegard's victims were both men and women, but he preferred women by far – and especially if they were attractive – because, besides swindling them, he also seduced them. One of his first conquests was his children's baby-sitter. He played the usual game with her: first the revelation of being an agent of the intelligence service, and then the threats. Her life was in danger because he had spent time with her, and they had been seen together in public . . . And so on. Thus when the girl became intimate with her employer, he took pictures of her naked, and when she tried to rebel, he threatened to show the compromising photos to her husband. He also imposed fidelity tests on the girl, challenging her with intelligence mission mind-games. For some time he terrified her so severely that she, under his orders, slept on a park bench at Heathrow airport and used the air terminal bathroom as though she were at home.

Soon he moved on to Newcastle, where he seduced another woman, and once again, giving quite detailed reasons, he asked her for money. The intelligence mission he described consisted of a series of operations to follow IRA killers who had been released under the Good Friday Agreement. He told the young woman that he had spent all the money MI5 had assigned to him, but that he was unable to get back in contact with his supervisor for security reasons. She gave him a thousand pounds. He said that it would be returned at the end of the operation.

Eleven on Ten

Seven women eventually reported Hendy-Freegard and were prepared to appear in court to testify against him. In reality, however, investigators suspect that there were probably many more women who did not have the courage to come forward, either out of modesty or shame, or because they actually loved the man. All seven who spoke out against him admitted to being seduced by his powers of persuasion and his assiduous courtship: he was tender, patient and affectionate with them. Most explicit was the account of a lawyer, Caroline Cowper, who without mincing words declared that on a sexual performance scale of 1 to 10, he scored 11. They had met in 2000, in a Chrysler dealership in West London, where she had gone to buy a car. After discussing the pros and cons of leasing versus buying, there was a brief courtship, and they became lovers, and he convinced her to become part of his intelligence service. In 2002, he seduced Kim Adams, a children's psychologist, after her stepfather had won a large prize in the lottery. He asked the young woman to move to an isolated lighthouse — for security reasons, of course.

When she refused, he told her that she could expect a bill for 80,000 pounds from the State, because in the meantime, since hiring her as a spy, he had already purchased the building for them. Kim's stepfather lent her the money.

Arrest and Two Trials

In the end, Hendy-Freegard was unmasked. He was arrested in the company of Kim Adams. After she, like the others, had severed relationships with her family for security reasons, Robert allowed her to meet her mother on the condition that she come back with 10,000 pounds for her espionage training. For a certain period the (real) police and Scotland Yard tapped his telephone and followed him. When he landed at the airport with Kim, besides her mother, he found the police waiting to arrest him.

WITHOUT REMORSE OR COMPASSION

After the defendant was found guilty of more than twenty crimes, including kidnapping, fraud, seduction of a minor, violence, theft, and using a false identity in the usurpation of a title, Judge Deva Pillay of the Blackfriars Crown Court sentenced Robert Hendy-Freegard to life in prison. In the verdict, Pillay described Hendy-Freegard as "egotistical and opinionated confidence trickster who has shown not a shred of remorse nor compassion for the degradation and suffering to which your victims were subjected." The magistrate, after listening for eight months to the testimonies of men and women who believed the incredible stories of Robert Hendy-Freegard, and who had handed over to him, among other things, approximately one million pounds, admitted almost with admiration: "He is a man endowed with devious charm." The man's charm, devious or not, proved effective two years later when the Appeals Court cut his life sentence down to a modest nine years.

After a trial that lasted many months, the Blackfriars Crown Court found Robert Hendy-Freegard guilty. In June of 2005 he was sentenced to life in prison. Two years later, a court of appeals dismissed the kidnapping charge, and reduced the sentence to nine years.

The Jäger Collection

Wolfgang and Helene Fischer (Germany)

Wolfgang and Helene. He was a hippy who became a professional forger. She played the part of a mysterious heiress. Both were so convincing that they deceived, for almost twenty years, critics, dealers, and collectors, accumulating a fortune they invested in luxury, travel, and, following their discovery, every effort at staying atop the crest of the wave of their success.

On May 8th, 2015, the Munich gallery Art room9 inaugurated a exhibition titled *Freedom*. The name might appear to be unoriginal but for the fact that the focus of the exhibition was a painter who had just been released from prison: Wolfgang Beltracchi, originally Wolfgang Fischer, born in 1951 in Höxter, Germany. Beltracchi was the surname of his wife Helene, who was sentenced along with him. In 2011 they confessed to forging and selling fourteen paintings attributed to Max Ernst, Heinrich Campendonk, Max Pechstein, Fernand Léger, and Kees van Dongen. These forgeries, which ended up in great collections, increased the Fischer-Beltracchi family wealth by about 16 million euros.

A Real Hippy

For Wolfgang, art had always been a craft more than a vocation. He was the son of a restaurateur and church decorator, and grew up watching his father attempting to imitate the most diverse techniques and styles: Mr. Fischer had to repair the battered paintings that were entrusted to his care and, occasionally, to make copies of masterpieces of the past.

He seemed bound to follow his father's craft, but unenthusiastically and discontentedly. Wolfgang's seventeenth birthday, however, coincided with 1968, the year of dreams and protests. Expelled from school, he enrolled at the Werkkunstschule in Aachen, where he spent more time in pubs and nightclubs than in the classroom. His life began to move in a completely different direction.

In Munich in the 1970s, Wolfgang took part in collective shows and obtained some praise from the critics. But his earnings were low, and no one follows a trade unless it is worth it: otherwise, he might just as well stay in his father's workshop. It was better to travel around on a Harley Davidson, enjoying life on Spanish communes, Moroccan beaches and houseboats moored in the canals of Amsterdam, waiting for his next brilliant idea. This took its time coming, despite attempts to stimulate it with marijuana and LSD.

This photo showing Wolfgang Fischer and his wife has the composition of a painting.

From Dutch Landscapes to German Expressionism

In the end, the eureka moment came while he was strolling in local markets and antiquarians' shops. Wolfgang observed how eighteenth-century winter landscapes sold for much higher prices when they included figures skating on ice. And so it was a short step to purchasing bare landscapes and "correcting" the subjects by cleverly adding some skaters. He'd then sell the paintings for increased prices. Wolfgang decided to become an out-and-out forger. But he did not like hard work: he dropped Flemish and Dutch art, which required studies on pigments and binders used in various eras, historical research, and great caution regarding possible anachronisms in the subjects. He chose a simpler and more profitable way: the twentieth-century *avant garde*, in particular the French Fauves and the German Expressionists.

Helene's Role

In 1992, when he met Helene Beltracchi, Wolfgang's business was going quite well. He had just bought a sailboat on which he intended to sail the seven seas. Obviously, at others' expense: he had obtained financing with the pretext of shooting a documentary on pirate adventures.

Helene and Wolfgang fell in love. Even before they married, they became a working couple. It was she, with her great experience in collaborating with an antique dealer, who transformed her husband's business into nothing less than an industry. She acted as an intermediary with auction houses and galleries, placing the forgeries with incredible coolness. When it was necessary, she became a talented actress: in fact, in order to explain the large number of paintings she possessed, she began to play the part of an heiress. She claimed that her maternal grandfather, Werner Jäger, had left her a large collection. For a long time, her family kept the collection a secret because it had been purchased by taking advantage of Alfred Flechtheim (a Jewish gallery owner and collector who really existed) in the first years of the Nazi regime. She went so far as to dress up in nineteen-forties clothes and play the role of a fictitious grandmother, Josefine, in a photograph that Wolfgang arranged in front of the masterpieces of the Jäger Collection, which were obviously all copies. The image, artfully aged, became a trump card, as was the biased testimony of her mother, her sister Jeannette, and her friend Otto Schulte-Kellinghaus, who presented himself with the credentials of a rich baron.

Nearing the End – a New Beginning

In 1995, the winds began to change. An expert opinion commissioned by a suspicious collector reached the conclusion that some of the paintings sold as works of Johannes Molzahn were in fact forgeries. When the police took Otto Schulte-Kellinghaus in for questioning, Wolfgang sensed the danger.

He and Helene moved to France, where they purchased and restored the splendid estate of Domaine des Rivettes, surrounded by vineyards and olive groves and not far from Montpellier. He began a long period of parties, travel and luxury, placing, meanwhile, new forgeries on the international circuit, works for which he received enormous sums.

His paintings were so convincingly executed that they deceived even the ex-director of the Centre Pompidou in Paris, Werner Spies, and Dorothea Tanning, Max Ernst's widow, who considered Wolfgang's copy of Ernst's *La Forêt* authentic, estimating its value at almost 2 million euros.

In the meantime, the German investigation came to nothing. In 2005, Fischer felt safe enough to move into a fabulous house in Freiburg. Very probably, it was there that he painted the picture that would put an end to his career: *Rotes Bild mit Pferden* (*Red Picture with Horses*), a false Campendonk dated 1914, which in 2006 was sold to a Maltese company for almost 3 million euros. What made the buyers suspicious was the back of the painting, where Fischer had stuck a label with the name and logo of the Flechtheim Collection (from which, according to Helene's story, the work had been transferred to the Jäger Collection). The logo was quite different from those found on other paintings really owned by Flechtheim. The painting was then subjected to scientific analysis and the tests left no room for doubt: the painting contained a pigment, titanium white, which in 1914 was not yet commercially available.

In August, 2010, Wolfgang and Helene were arrested. At the trial, he was sentenced to six years in prison and she to four (but they would serve only half of these sentences); they also had to return the money they'd illegally earned for the forgeries.

There is no doubt that many more than the fourteen paintings to which the accused pleaded guilty remain in circulation. The authorities expressed their suspicions about more than fifty works, even though the couple implied that they had sold hundreds of paintings, some of which were hanging in famous museums. A further confession would be in no one's interest: neither the museums' nor the collectors', who would risk seeing the value of their collections depreciate. Nor would another confession be in the interest of the fooled experts and dealers: they would risk a sensational loss of credibility. Wolfgang and Helene knew this very well, and seemed to enjoy terrifying the art establishment.

THE INTERVIEW

In a March, 2012, interview with the German weekly *Der Spiegel*, Wolfgang Fischer Beltracchi stated: "Fame never interested me. I could have exhibited more of my own works in the 1970s, but I didn't want to. It's sort of like being a child. When you're finished with school, you have only one thing on your mind: to get out and experience life. Did I want to spend all my time working on a painting? No, I wanted to have fun, travel, meet women and live life." When asked whether he had ever been tempted to tell to the world that some paintings considered to be masterpieces were in fact his, and whether he had ever thought of signing the forgeries with a hidden sign, a sort of code message, he replied: "With one Max Ernst, it did briefly cross my mind to incorporate a Mickey Mouse into the painting. But the people who did that sort of thing usually didn't remain in the business for long."

What is certain is that it was negligence that betrayed Wolfgang Fischer Beltracchi. He was wrong to assume that forging twentieth-century art did not require painstaking work of historic, technical and scientific preparation, and wrong to assume that psychological identification with the artist and pure talent would be enough. Today Wolfgang admits ironically that for the first time in his life, at retirement age, he is forced to work. He says he has run out of money and is still millions of euros in debt. Nevertheless, his paintings, now signed with given and family names, sell extremely well, which is also due to Helene's management of his image. His first show, in fact, brought in more than 600,000 euros. So in his way, Wolfgang has become a star: there are books and documentaries about him. And, despite his time in prison, he has not lost either his hippy charm or his ready wit. When asked whether he would do it again, he replied:

No. Certainly not... I wouldn't use titanium white.

Cursed 419 Times

James Adebayo and many others (Nigeria)

It is a dream we share: to change our destiny by anticipating the future, by being more clever than the next guy. For some it is the lottery, for others a scratch-card. Others use a gun. Still others wait for that special proposal in the mail – and end up throwing their savings to the wind, begging for help from a loan shark. Behind the computer screen lurk professional swindlers, "the fox and the cat" of the twenty-first century.

Marco Giorgetti, an average Joe, closed the lid of his laptop and stared vacantly into the distance, breathing deeply. A million euros. A million euros by simply investing 10,000 euros. "Certainly," he thought. "Where can I find 10,000 euros right now? Who has that kind of money? My bank account's in the red, I haven't worked for six months, Carla's doing those heavy

shifts at the call-center, I have to get Francesca and Peter to school
– so long as I'm free . . . But how much does it cost every day,
for books, papers? five euros for a trip, ten for a birthday gift for
a classmate . . . And if you don't help them out then the kid is
marked forever at school." It's for the kids, for Carla . . . Marco
could not pass up the opportunity of getting his hands on a million euros. If he didn't, someone else would. Otherwise, there was
The Hop, a few blocks away. A loan shark, call him what you will,
but if The Hop lent him the 10,000, even at an exorbitant rate
of interest, his worries would be over forever. For Carla, no more
call-center, Francesca and Peter, new jackets, new shoes, and they
could take that Caribbean vacation they'd been talking about all
these years. "Who knows . . . Francesca and Peter, they could go
to whatever school they wanted. Money will never be a problem."

He was sweating. It was winter, and he'd lowered the thermo-
stat to save a penny, and it was cold in the house. But he was sweating. He opened his laptop. His English was good, a little scholastic
but correct, better than the other guy's. James Adebayo, writing
from Abuja, Nigeria, used colloquialisms and some jargon that he
wasn't familiar with. What counts is that the message is clear.

What Is 25% of 4 Million?

"Dear Sir," wrote Mr. Adebayo, a former minister of labor, "you
are probably wondering why I contacted you." Thus began the
message, and thus began Marco Giorgetti's journey toward hope.
The former minister directed a benevolent foundation, and had
to urgently send 4 million dollars to Italy for a medical operation
that must be done on some children in a clinic in Rome. He had
gone through his embassy but they could not complete certain

---

*This swindle began in Nigeria and was given the name of "419 scam" from the number of
the penal code of the African country.*

trade operations. His only hope – and the only way those children were going to get the surgery they needed – was to ask help "from a person of good will" who had an Italian bank account. The commission, guaranteed by Nigerian law, was 25%. Adebayo had attached the text of the law, there was no doubt. Giorgetti read the line for the hundredth time, and for the hundredth time did the calculation: 25% of 4 million is one million.

Certainly, he had to contact a notary public, but Mr. Adebayo would have taken care of that. The only problem was to antici-pate lawyers expenses and shipment, fees totaling 10,000 euros. But what was 10,000 euros compared to a sum that could change his life? Better not to talk to Carla yet . . . Surprise her when it's all over. Giorgetti copied on his cell phone the data to enable him to send the ex-minister 10,000 euros via Western Union. Then he closed the laptop and set off for The Hop's house. The die was cast.

An Upset and Little Indignant Diplomat

"We are very upset, Mr. Giorgetti. Upset and – let me add – also a little indignant." The ministerial advisor at the Nigerian embassy spoke admirable Italian. The pinstripe suit was hardly stretched over the slight swelling of the man's belly, falling smoothly around his red-purple necktie. Giorgetti instead was completely depressed, his eyes shifting from the diplomat to the police in-spector who has accompanied him. In his eyes there is no longer any trace of hope. "We are indignant because this scam continues to be associated with our country, even if nowadays only a frac-tion of such e-mails actually comes from Nigeria."

The inspector nodded in agreement and Giorgetti sank lower in his seat. It was all lost. The 10,000 euros had vanished, swal-

AN OUTLINE OF THE "419 SCAM"

The Nigerian swindle is a modern version of an old trick. It involves the swindler's need to ship money or goods to a place he cannot access; thus the role of the mark, an ingenuous soul who's willing to help in exchange for an enormous (though obviously fictitious) sum. Spanish prisoners in the seventeenth century did it, smugglers in the colonial era did it, and traffickers through the Iron Curtain did it.

In the age of the internet (after 1994), swindlers attempting this scam often assume a name that sounds African, like Agbaje Kamoru, Alex Owogold, or Ayobami Ogunsan. Sometimes the swindler hides behind the fictitious identity of a celebrity or public authority, like Suha Arafat, wife of the former Palestinian leader, or Williams Gumbeze, son of one of the richest men in Zimbabwe. With an email, they lure into the net someone willing to take the bait of a promise of a dizzying percentage in exchange for helping to transfer money or goods from one country to another. The only problem – as the narrative for this scam goes – is a small sum that has to be paid in advance, and though the sum seems significant, it's also trivial in comparison with the much larger amount promised in the end. It is believed that the scam originates in Nigeria, although today it has gone global. Another name for the fraudulent practice is the "419 scam," from article 419 of the Nigerian criminal code: undue profit through false pretenses and deceit is punishable by up to three years in prison.

lowed up by the emptiness beyond the screen at the Western Union internet point he'd used. There were no former ministers by the name of James Adebayo, and the Nigerian embassy had no record of its citizens participating in any medical programs intended to help children, nor knowledge of any foundations dedicated to such things. The shadow of The Hop was already looming. It was one detail he couldn't tell the inspector.

Giorgetti trembled in his seat. The worst thing was not knowing who was on the other side of the screen. The dark mass that had swallowed his money and his future, it hid an undefined threat. It is as if there were a monster that can jump out from the darkness from one moment to the next.

"I can't believe it," the inspector told his wife that evening, as they had supper in front of the TV. "How is it possible that there are still people who fall for a trick like that?"

"People never change," observed his wife with a shrug. "It's the story of the fox and the cat, like in Pinocchio."

Beyond the Mediterranean

A fiber-optic cable runs under the Mediterranean. It branches out into thousands of similar cables, one of which slips beneath the Sahara and races towards the Niger delta, where it then launches itself like a dolphin beyond the Gulf of Guinea, across the Atlantic towards the American continent, carrying its infinite load of bits that are regrouped at intermediate stations to form love letters, news reports, sports stories, and bank transfer codes.

THREATENING MESSAGES

Police archives all over the world contain e-mail messages very similar to the following: "We received a fax from our World-wide Commando in New York this morning. We inform you that you must send us the sum of $35,000 USD (thirty-five thousand U.S. dollars) through our account in Switzerland indicated below in the next ninety-six (96) hours. If this does not happen, we will kidnap you and force you to commit suicide during the celebration of the fiftieth anniversary of our Commando." A 2010 victim of such a threat told the police: "In a few seconds my life was in absolute chaos. Suddenly I was receiving calls from everywhere in the world, from Afghanistan, India, Africa, Washington. They were anxious friends and people I knew as journalists in foreign offices. They'd heard that something had happened."

At a cyber café in Port Harcourt two lean and gangly men, in faded jeans and large Barcelona and Manchester United t-shirts, stuffed two creased envelopes in their pockets. These contained more than a million naira each, approximately 5000 euros a head. They looked around suspiciously. The area was not the most reassuring. Through the smashed-in door of a two-story adobe house they caught a glimpse in the darkness inside of someone, and the man in the Barcelona shirt repressed a shiver. He thought he'd seen Cripple, known as "The Hop", to whom he owed a fair amount of money. Now he could pay it back. But hunger came with eating, and the money he'd torn from the stupid Italian had a hold on him. There was always time to pay back Cripple.

On the other side of the city a man with salt-and-pepper hair held an unlit cigarette tightly in his teeth. "I gotta stop smoking," he said, while a crooked smile formed on his lips. He sat in front of a computer. He was the chief of police in Port Harcourt. The new program that traced electronic money transfers was beginning to yield results. Called "Operation Eagle Claw," it was launched by Nigerian authorities in collaboration with no less an authority than Microsoft.

"We have a 419," he said to his partner, crushing the cigarette in his fist. Article 419 of the Nigerian criminal code: enrichment through false pretenses and deceit. For the Italian, there'd be a happy ending. For many, it could be much worse: some victims were persuaded to travel to Nigeria and end up kidnapped by gangs far more dangerous than these two scarecrows. "Come on," said the chief, "let's pick these two up. The fox and the cat, like in Pinocchio."

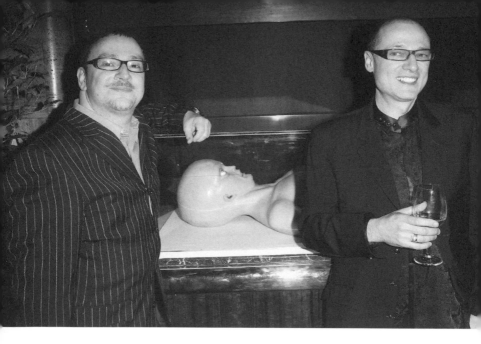

Alien Autopsy

Ray Santilli and Gary Shoefield
(United States)

Once upon a time aliens, and everything related to them, were all the rage: they were in the cinema, on TV, in the news, everywhere. And everyone wanted to hear more about the most recent discovery, cover-up, and testimony. There was no limit to just how fantastic, or downright bizarre, these stories could be, and people everywhere, regardless of age, social class, or location, fell for them. Nobody was immune. In 1995, a British music producer of Italian origins, Ray Santilli, organized a kind of perfect trap for the media which, credulous and amenable in ways we haven't seen since, came forward with cameras rolling, no questions asked.

With an honorable career behind him in pop-rock, Santilli was the head of AMP Entertainment, an agency founded by himself that looked after the interests of artists and groups with established reputations (Bill Wyman, Leo Sayer, Sweet, Slade, Uriah Heep, Kid Creole and the Coconuts, among others). Born in 1960 in the London borough of Islington, Santilli expanded into the world of television by setting up a company, the Merlin Group, that would find itself at the center of a famous case in 1995. Santilli, in fact, announced he had come into possession of a disturbing film showing an autopsy being performed on an alien: it was apparently part of a medical report from the famous 1947 incident at Roswell, New Mexico, about which ufologists had been arguing for years.

The body of the alien – recovered as evidence of an event that immediately entered the catalog of fantastic mysteries –

THE ROSWELL SWINDLE

It is enough to read contemporary reports to get a clear idea: stories in all the papers, official army notices, airtime on the radio, dozens of military, civilian, adult and child witnesses, and strange debris turning up everywhere in the desert. Then the mobilization of the army, everything denied or comment refused, everything hushed-up quickly. First the Pentagon, then even the FBI were on the scene. And then the usual allegations followed; and the suspicious deaths; and evidence of the witnesses read *post mortem* by the notaries.

The basic story: a flying saucer crashed in Roswell, New Mexico, on the night of July 2nd, 1947. Found in the desert, among the hull of the ship and scattered debris, were the bodies of three-foot tall, humanoid beings with large heads. One of the creatures survived the crash and was taken to a hospital, where it was promptly removed by a team of soldiers. Obviously everything disappeared onto military trucks. Then the spin doctors went to work, quickly rewriting everything: it was only an army weather balloon that had landed. Everyone believes what they want. What is certain is that the official version sounded like a scam, a two-bit show.

From left, Shoefield and Santilli after the world premiere of the film Alien Autopsy, *on April 3rd, 2006, in London.*

was supposed to have been examined by a medical team to get information about a topic we know practically nothing about: namely, the nature of extra-terrestrials. The film, the results of the autopsy, and the identity of the professionals involved had been kept secret until the discovery of Santilli. The producer then filled in some of the details of the story, providing the name of the camera operator, Jack Barnett, the make of camera used – a Bells & Howell – and further details about the location of the shooting, all to lend credibility to the report.

Santilli's work was corroborated by an AFP report on March 27th, 1995, that summarized the story of the flying saucer and the body of the extra-terrestrial that was immediately removed by USAF staff to military laboratories, where a cameraman was on hand to document everything.

The journalist's reconstruction referred to a black and white, silent, 16 mm film that lasted ninety-one minutes. It was exactly what the eighty-two-year-old Jack Barnett had offered Santilli. Furthermore, according to the report, technicians in a Kodak lab had examined the film and dated it to approximately the late 1940s, early 1950s. Few had seen the film. It was said to contain shocking and disturbing images.

The high-profile news release that Santilli orchestrated bounced around the world, causing amazement and excitement on TV networks in many countries. There was then a rush to bid for the rights to transmit fifteen or so minutes, an ideal situation for Santilli and his Merlin Group. Figures of tens of millions of dollars were mentioned: the motor of the film marketing machine was working at full steam.

Background Noise

There were more than forty countries that had acquired the rights for the work. Santilli, for his part, the subject of endless

A SENSATIONAL FILM

What does an alien look like? The one shown on the film has an anthropomorphic aspect but includes decidedly alarming features: it has a spherical head, a triangular face without musculature, large entirely black eyes, hands with six fingers and feet with six toes. Its distended belly contains unrecognizable organs. The brain matter in the skull, opened with a hand saw, is also equally puzzling. The body is completely hairless. It has nipples and a navel, but no sexual attributes. It is like a manikin, filled up with animal entrails. The film had been shot in the recent past. Like many old documentaries, the film was of poor quality: its picture was blurred and out-of-focus, in grainy black and white, without much definition. The manikin occupied the center of the frame, but some conflicting technical details suggested artifice. The film was studied closely: many were not convinced by the low quality of the film, a significant number considered the alien "biological nonsense," and there was a complete lack of authenticity about the instruments used in the autopsy, about the medical procedure itself, and even about the filming, which was unorthodox and amateurish. For these reasons, the fact that the fraud circulated for so many years is nothing short of miraculous: the desire for sensationalism, and the fascination with conspiracy theories and referrals to suspect personalities operating in the shadows, played an important role in this. Additionally, there was the indulgence and encouragement of the generalists' science that often typifies ufology. Who came off worst, however, were the more serious and committed ufologists, who derived no benefit from so ham-fisted an adventure. After an initial phase of interest, many turned to demolishing the story with point by point critical analysis. For example, Philip Mantle, a well known British investigator who was one of the first to see the film, published a 318-page book, *Roswell Alien Autopsy: The Truth Behind The Film That Shocked The World*.

articles and interviews, spoke freely about the film, claiming that it would become "the Turin Shroud of Ufology." That is, a puzzle without end, a maze where skeptic and believer would be lost together.

The appearance of the alien – photos and clips of which can be found today in many places, including YouTube – turned out to be rather alarming: the carbonized right leg, the swollen belly, the lack of sexual organs, the humanoid face with eyes that create a certain uneasiness. It is an injured E.T., in short. The quickly advanced hypothesis of a hoax was opposed by the cross-fire of Santilli and his supporters. And the opinions of several surgeons and technical and professional experts who explained the weak points of the production were to little avail: the influence of the media operation remained strong.

Adding to the avalanche of the production's success was a strong publicity campaign for the release of an English film entitled *Alien Autopsy* (2006) – starring a comic duo, Ant & Dec, the television actors Anthony McPartlin and Declan Donnelly – for which Santilli was executive producer.

Faith, Hope, and Delight

As the speculators advance, the uncontrollable wave of enthusiasm they depend on is finally met by the inquiries and curiosities of the reporters. A special program on British Sky showed discrepancies and contradictions in Santilli's film. In response, Santilli and his friend Gary Shoefield prepared an alternative version of the film. They claimed that they had saved only a few frames of the original twenty-two rolls shot and delivered to them in 1993, and that they had created a meticulous reconstruction using a mock-up in latex, a "manufactured" prop made by an artist at the Royal Academy, John Humphreys. (It had been filled with animal entrails.) Additionally, the cameraman, Jack Barnett – shown in an interview that was later sold to a Japanese TV program – was not the original cameraman, but a stand-in, a former actor who they'd found sleeping on the streets of Los Angeles (The real cameraman, naturally, wanted to protect his anonymity, to avoid excessive harassment.) The film, with the set transformed into a hospital laboratory, was made in Santilli's London apartment in Camden Town; certain editing techniques let them mix authentic images with new footage, making it impossible to detect splicing in the film.

The story, which had its fair share of trapdoors and mirror-games, had surprises to come. In 2007, in a further twist, an Anglo-Cypriot illusionist, Spyros Melaris, claimed that he had been duped by Santilli. Melaris claimed that he had been commissioned to direct a film that would have no ties with anything original, or any film from 1947. Giving force and substance to his allegations, he sketched the storyboard, provided the names and roles of the production team, and offered various details which only someone well-informed and on the inside of the production would know. The new wave of revelations was aimed at exposing agreements not respected by Santilli. The producer, apparently, had promised Melaris a share of the rights and more than 10,000 pounds on delivery of the final edit. The dispute would become ruinous, putting the overall structure of the scam at more risk than ever.

The Debate Continues

After twelve years, Santilli's scheme seemed to have been definitively dismantled. So was the adventure over? Not exactly, because the debate to verify how Santilli fabricated the so-called "original" material continued, and continues. A DVD was released: *Alien from Area 51-The Alien Autopsy Footage Revealed*. It includes twenty minutes of exclusive interviews with Santilli and Shoefield, who fire some large caliber shots: they describe the threats they received, the Chinese who knew all about the original 1947 film, the visits of aliens, the genetic mutations, the governments who manage the information and the secrets . . .

Among the results triggered by Santilli's well-orchestrated media storm are tens of millions of spectators in the United States alone, debates raised among experts of every school, questions for two Oscar winning special effects experts (Stan Winston, *Aliens*, and Carl Rambaldi, the father of E.T.), and citations in video-clips that have even appeared in a pair of *X-Files* episodes.

Among so much criticism and controversy, the reckless and laid back Santilli has received one prize. *Scienza & Paranormale*, a magazine published by Cicap (the Italian Committee for Inspecting Paranormal Events) awarded him the "Gold Buffalo" in April of 1996, with the citation:

For successfully selling his product to half the world.

The Republic of Eden

Clyde D. Hood (United States)

Mattoon, a sleepy little town of 15,000 in the heart of Illinois, half-way between Springfield and Indianapolis, was like many provincial American towns in the 1990s: its economy was in decline, its graduates were leaving for the cities, and its population was getting old. Clyde D. Hood, an electrician, was having a hard time making ends meet. He needed to do something to help himself, but also, he felt, he had to help the community. Then one morning he had an idea, and he couldn't get it out of his head . . .

In 1994, Clyde D. Hood, sixty years old, a retired electrician, found himself with a lot of free time on his hands. One morning, he had a brilliant entrepreneurial idea that, according to him, was not the product of economic reasoning but of divine illumination. He was chosen by God to carry out a mission. The first people he told about his idea were, naturally, his fellow parishioners. The project had to do with exploiting a feature of the web – then in its infancy – and thus becoming rich. So he founded Omega Trust and Trading Ltd. Although the company was nothing more than an internet portal, he invited potential micro-investors to take part in a gigantic "humanitarian operation" through which it would be possible to make extraordinary profits. Hood guaranteed a return multiplied by 51 to anyone investing in Omega Trust: thus, in 275 days he promised to pay back 5100 dollars for every 100 dollars of initial contribution.

Hood convinced his investors that what appeared improbable on paper was in fact a likely outcome, strengthening the confidence the people of his provincial town placed in him. He boasted that he was an international trader in contact with Wall Street bankers, men who knew everything about stocks and bonds. For this reason, he said, he could make such safe and profitable investments that he would able to repay 5000% of the initial capital. Moreover, Hood also promised to use the investments to finance unspecified "charitable" work.

The shrewd electrician asked his clients to purchase shares, at least a 100 dollars' worth, to be sent (only in cash, and wrapped in aluminum foil so as to prevent them from being stolen) through Federal Express (the U.S. Postal Service would not deliver bank bills in the mail). Obviously, secrecy was required of the "stockholders" to avoid irritating the experts in the banks who were Hood's so-called advisors. His plan was simple, and the investment

---

A smiling Clyde D. Hood, the self-proclaimed and undisputed leader of the Free Republic of Eden.

he asked for was modest: people trusted him. All his investors had to do was send him their money. In essence, it was a model which resembled both the Charles Ponzi scheme and the pyramid one, which guaranteed high interest returns to the first investors, so long as further investments continued. At least, the returns would materialize until the mechanism broke down.

A Shower of Dollars

The FedEx offices in Mattoon were literally flooded with envelopes from all over the states, and then from countries and regions all over the globe: Honduras, Australia, Europe, China, and Canada. The envelopes contained the same thing: small-denomination bank bills, sent by people who believed it was possible to multiply their investment by 5000. In the first year, Hood collected about 10 million dollars. It was an unexpected figure that forced Hood to pause operations and not accept any new partners. In reality, Omega Trust "partners" hadn't seen a single dollar returned. Hood cited "international geopolitics," unanticipated "administrative expenses," and "problems with foreign banks" to gain time. But the pressure of those wanting to invest led to the re-opening of the program. Soon shares in the company were selling for well over a hundred dollars, each of these paid in cash. When Omega Trust was definitively shut down, Hood had more money (20 million dollars, cash) than he knew what to do with.

An Advantage for Everyone

As swindles go, Hood's scheme had a rare feature: the socialization of the booty. He shared a substantial part of the money with some of the people of Mattoon. In fact, although the elec-

In the creation of the brilliantly successful scam, Hood, probably unconsciously, exploited a widespread feeling in the world: suspicion of finance institutions. Hood's secret, and the key to the fabulous earnings he promised, was his link "with the great bankers who plot in the shadows." This connection was seen by many uninformed people as a guarantee of success, because of the commonly held opinion that the world of finance is murky and controlled by the few who know in advance what will happen and how to earn from it. Not that this is not partially true – various investigations in the last few years have revealed just this – but the difference between suspecting that not everything is above board, and sending bank bills in an envelope to a stranger who promises easy riches, is the same difference that exists between a careful consumer and, as they say, a "sucker."

trician was suddenly a very rich man, he couldn't declare his earnings to the IRS. Moreover, the entire town knew about the envelopes coming into the local FedEx office. So Hood, honoring his promise to finance "charitable projects," turned out to be a very generous man. But his charity wasn't charity in the common sense of the word, helping the weakest groups in society: rather, he offered loans, at very low interest rates, to those public figures in town who would take the money without asking too many questions.

Thus the sheriff fulfilled his dream of starting a vintage car collection, a restaurateur opened a new, luxurious restaurant, the church minister bought himself a brand-new Harley-Davidson, and a pastry chef opened a pretzel factory. In all, eighteen people in Mattoon benefited from the former electrician's scheme.

The Republic of Eden

Mattoon was coming back. The economy was growing, the people were happy: it was as if all of a sudden this little provincial town in the middle of Illinois had turned into the Garden of Eden. It was just this name that Hood, by then nearly seventy years old, used to talk about his city, printing letterheads which proclaimed him the undisputed leader of the "Free Republic of Eden" His wife became the First Lady. And as happens in every nation, Mattoon's self-proclaimed leader appointed confident diplomatic representatives – the most skeptical investors, the readiest to claim their rights – to be sent around the United States or abroad as ambassadors. It was a farcical aspect to the scam, but one which Hood took seriously, perhaps showing the first signs of mental instability. When a public prosecutor went to Mattoon to learn more about how various citizens had become so rich so quickly, Hood told him:

> *That is not the business of the United States government. This is a sovereign republic.*

Hood's response to the prosecutor's questions marked the beginning of the end for the Mattoon electrician and his accomplices. The prosecutor reported them to the SEC, the financial supervisory body in the United States, because he was suspicious about both Hood's entrepreneurial initiative and the man's passionate political ambition.

In January, 2002, Hood was sentenced to fourteen years in prison for crimes ranging from money laundering to aggravated fraud. His fellow citizens got off with heavy fines and the restitution of the assets acquired from the proceeds of the fraud.

In the end, however, Hood never went to prison: he served, in fact, his sentence at the Effingham Rehabilitation & Health Care Center, a center specialized in the care of Alzheimer's disease. When he died in 2012, his dream of an earthly Eden went with him.

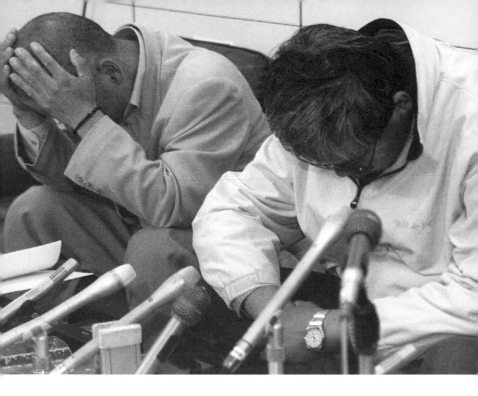

The Hand of God

Shin'ichi Fujimura (Japan)

Japan has always been isolated, and cannot boast a remote past like the rest of the Asian continent. The oldest archeological evidence in the archipelago dates from just 30,000 years ago. But an amateur archeologist, Shin'ichi Fujimura, made it his business to correct the text books and enrich the collections of museums. For twenty years, he cleverly modified excavation sites, retro-dating evidence of human activity in his country by some hundreds of thousands of years.

I t's not just the money. The forging of artistic objects, antiques, and even archeological evidence may not strictly be motivated by venality. Forgers sometimes act in order to answer a desire for personal success, out of vanity, or sometimes to satisfy the mythopoetic needs of a culture or nation. All of these elements contribute to the singular story of a man who, for a long period, for good or ill, was a successful and very popular Japanese archeologist. Shin'ichi Fujimura was born in 1950 in Kami, in the Miyagi Prefecture, north of Tokyo. From childhood, when he found in the courtyard of his home some fragments of Jomon ceramics (dating from about 12,000 B.C.), he cultivated a passion for antiquity. After high school, he took a post in an electronics company, but his interest was completely directed towards Japanese prehistory. In 1972, he began to teach himself archeology, and to devote his vacations to research into Paleolithic artifacts.

It Was Time to Rewrite the History Books

In 1975, Fujimura, with other amateurs and several academics, founded the archeological society Sekki Bunka Kenkyukai. They organized digs in the Miyagi Prefecture. These were successful projects: between 1981 and 1984, in the sites of Zazaragi, Nakamine and Babadan, Fujimura, using stratigraphic analysis, discovered stoneware and ceramics that were about 50,000 years old. For the scientific community, this was a shock: in fact, the finds proved to be almost twice as old as the oldest Japanese artifact discovered until then. It was also an exciting discovery for the country: while on the Asian continent archeologists had discovered sites going back hundreds of thousands of years, evidence of human society in Japan was no more than 30,000 years old, when, following the refinement of navigation techniques, people from the Korean coast first colonized the archipelago.

Shin'ichi Fujimura during the press conference of November 6th, 2000.

For the Japanese, the idea of having such a limited past was vaguely humiliating, and still worse was the fact of their land was first colonized by Korea. So when the Fujimura discoveries significantly retro-dated human presence in Japan, it awakened national pride: it was time to rewrite the textbooks! The need to revise the chronology of the Paleolithic Age almost became a litany. Following the first finds, Fujimura supplied new discoveries, evidence of even more ancient societies, revealing an extraordinary instinct for a person without significant training in archeology, geology, or paleoanthropology. Fujimura turned up so much evidence, in fact, that he earned the nickname "the hand of God", and an appointment at the prestigious Tohoku Institute.

With twenty years in the profession, and 180 archeological campaigns behind him, Fujimura almost became a national hero. The press adored him, and the academic world, for the most part, avoided questioning his work. He had a few critics. In 1986, the archeologists Shizuo Oda and Charles T. Keally wrote that "the discoveries of the Early Paleolithic in the Miyagi Prefecture are based on inaccurate research" and that "there is no evidence of artifacts before 30,000 B.C." In 1998, another archeologist, Toshiki Takeoka, of the Kyoritsu Joshi University, questioned Fujimura's evidence, describing the finds as Ooparts (an acronym for Out of Place Artifacts). But Fujimura continued to work undisturbed and to achieve further success. He was so popular that the locations of his excavation campaigns became popular with tourists. For example, the city of Tsukidate became the destination for many enthusiasts, and it was there that they even created a cocktail named after the primitive man.

The Real Discovery

The excesses of Fujimura's success finally condemned "the hand of God." In 2000, the skepticism of a journalist from the *Mainichi Shimbun* definitively broke the spell. It was the story of a child caught with his hand in the cookie jar: a single blow ended the career of the archeologist and a nation's dreams of glory. The journalist placed a hidden telecamera on the site where Fujimura was working, the Kamikatamori, and what it recorded was disconcerting. In the video, one clearly saw the archeologist extract pieces of ceramic from a transparent bag and hide them in the excavation. The ceramics, of Asiatic origin, were ancient, and the stratigraphic examination according to Fujimura's plans would date them to around 570,000 years old. The textbooks would need to be rewritten yet again.

Fujimura's press conference was predictably sensational, but much greater was the scandal caused by the publication of the images in the Sunday edition of the newspaper. The archeologist was compelled to confess his misdeeds: to a packed press conference, and with a very different tone, Fujimura made a deep bow of shame, apologizing to the journalists and to the country:

I did something that I shouldn't have done. I had wanted to find more ruins that included stone artifacts.

It was the destruction of a myth, and an indefensible attack against an emerging national epic. The archeologist-forger initially admitted to manipulating evidence in only the last site, and doing it due to stress: he thus portrayed himself as a victim of the media. But subsequent verifications by archeologists (real ones) established that there were at least forty-two cases of fraud.

For some months, the press continued to publish revelations on Fujimura's false sites, and even identified an accomplice, Professor Mitsuo Kagawa, who, out of honor, wrote a letter protesting his innocence and killed himself. The court, in a lawsuit filed by the professor's family, would later rule that the magazine *Shukan Bunshun* must pay damages for libel.

Shin'ichi Fujimura did not commit suicide, but all of his "discoveries" were considered fraudulent, and, reduced from illustrious archeologist to forger, he was expelled from all associations. The reputation of the Tohoku Institute was also seriously damaged, as was, in general, the credibility of archeological science. Some museums, including the Tokyo National Museum, were compelled to withdraw the finds on display, and the history textbooks had to be rewritten for the last time, erasing forever the name of the ex-archeologist. The history of human society in Japan, the last edition of these books claim, does not date from half a million years ago but, according to archeological evidence, from no more than 30,000 years ago.

A LATE COLONIZATION

Ever since prehistoric times, Japan has been particularly isolated from the rest of the world. Its late colonization is partly due to this. The first written mention of its existence is found in a Chinese text of 50 B.C., the *Hou Hanshu*, which describes a "Wa people, formed of hundreds of tribes." Archeological excavations have dated the first cultivation of rice and the production of bronze in Japan to around 300 B.C., while the first semi-nomadic villages, with some traces of agriculture and the production of ceramics, date from the Jomon culture of the twelfth and thirteenth centuries B.C. The first finds by Shin'ichi Fujimura were from this period. As he became older, his desire to give Japan the glorious archeological past he thought it deserved drove him to create his sensational forgeries.

The Hyena of Wall Street

Bernard Madoff (United States)

He was a lifeguard at the beach, always on the lookout, anticipating need, weakness, overconfidence. The company he later built would become known, following the banking crisis of 2008, as one of the greatest scams in the history of finance (according to Forbes second only to that of Enron, the energy giant; or third, if we include the 24 hours millionaire of the IOR). But the tragedy of so much money lost would pale in comparison to what his family paid for his crimes.

The story of the financier Bernard Madoff has all the ingredients for a sequel to the Martin Scorsese's *The Wolf of Wall Street* (2013), and producers at HBO have turned it into a full length feature for the small screen (*The Wizard of Lies*, 2016) with Robert de Niro in the lead role. But, while having the same scam matrix as in the film of Scorsese, what Madoff did is completely different. The tycoon is the antithesis of the character played by Leonardo DiCaprio in the earlier film. No sex, no drugs, no eccentricity. On the contrary, a lot of apparent normality. Madoff – Bernie to his friends – was born into a New York Jewish family of Polish origin in 1938. It is not known whether he was acquainted early on with the old Jewish story of the merchant in debt: this merchant always worked at a loss, taking on, every day, more and more debt. He used credit from previous deals to barely stay afloat. One day, a friend tells him that sooner or later he's going to be found out, and he's going to sink. His answer?

With the grace of God, if I am lucky, I'll die when I'm at the very bottom.

A humble and contrite Bernard Madoff, after the verdict, on March 10th, 2009.

Genesis

Before opening Bernard L. Madoff Investment Securities LLC, the company he'd be president of until the day of his arrest, Madoff worked as a lifeguard in the Hamptons, the beach area for New York's upper classes at the eastern end of Long Island. To supplement his income he also installed sprinkler systems. With the savings from these two jobs, and with a loan from his father-in-law, he opened a brokerage company that supplied liquidity to people wanting to buy stocks and shares on the Stock Exchange. The company also had a team specializing in savings advice and management.

Following principles of his spiritual master, Charles Ponzi (an Italian immigrant to the United States in the early 1900's, who is remembered for the notorious "Ponzi Scheme," a cornerstone to many financial scams), Madoff identified in his own community the first targets for his operations. And so, while Ponzi aimed at Italian immigrants, Bernie found his customers in the Jewish community, among friends and acquaintances of his father-in-law. He even dedicated to them those securities that made his customers very rich, nicknaming them "Jewish Bond."

The Factory Brand

Unlike Ponzi, Madoff did not work with people devoid of any understanding of finance and investment. His customers were people of average expertise. So he studied the Ponzi scheme carefully, examining its weak points.

He did not promise yields of 400%, as his master had done; he limited himself to a more modest 10-12%. It was a high but credible percentage, even for those who knew little about finance: renouncing high yields generally means retaining more secure yields. But the true genius of Madoff was to purposefully complicate how potential customers accessed certain services provided by Bernard L. Madoff Investment Securities LLC. Potential customers were convinced that to have their money managed by this emerging financial strategist required diligent, unorthodox approaches. It was very difficult to get in, if not impossible. To be accepted, one had to be a friend of a friend, or had to have some connection to the elected magic circle, which was none other than the members of his family.

In order to give credibility to this daring strategy of not actively seeking clients, but leaving them to beg him to take their money, Madoff did not take part to the events of the high society. He had nothing to do with other New York investment managers. At the same time, he used a network of agents who worked the country club circuit and centers of exclusive associations, golf clubs, universities and banks in Europe . . . They traveled from Palm Beach to London on hunting expeditions for new potential investors, like the rich Italians, for example, with their nest eggs in Switzerland. Madoff's people, by the time of his arrest, had netted more than 5000 customers, among them VIPs like Steven Spielberg and Kevin Bacon and Jewish charitable associations like the Foundation of Elie Wiesel, philanthropist and Nobel peace-prize winner, survivor of the Nazi death camps. The money in these accounts was never invested or made to yield in any way. It ended up in a checking account in Chase Manhattan Bank (today J.P. Morgan & Co.), and was used by Madoff to return an investment or to distribute as a dividend to his customers.

THE LITURGY OF THE SWINDLE

Madoff knew how a good citizen ought to behave, and he followed these dictates scrupulously. He donated millions of dollars to various non-profit organizations. And, like many well-off Americans, he never forgot to contribute to electoral campaigns (in his case those of the Democrats).

His public persona was studied in detail. He also observed to the letter the liturgy that applied to the signing of contracts. For finalization, the "fortunate" investor was received by Madoff himself, in his office on the seventeenth floor of the Lipstick Building in the heart of Manhattan. Cool, confident and reassuring, in a Savile Row suit, he would promise modest, but certain yields. He explained that the activity of his brokerage house ranged from the negotiation of titles to the development of electronic trading platforms for shares and derivatives, for which he had the most prestigious companies on Wall Street, from Goldman Sachs to Merrill Lynch, as partners. "We begin with a small figure," he'd say, "and then, if we are both satisfied, we will pass on to something more substantial." It was a recommendation worth more than an increase in interest rates by a couple of points.

A Paper Castle

"It's too good to be true," said his detractors. Madoff's competitors began to have doubts about his operating practices already in as early as 2001: they could not explain how the financier managed to produce constant yields on the order of 15% a year, always guessing the best moment to buy and sell. But it was not their envy or their suspicions that caused Madoff's paper castle to collapse. Rather, it was the 2008 financial crisis, and collapse of the Lehman Brothers Bank, that brought unexpected pressure on Madoff. His customers were suddenly demanding their investments back and, to meet such demands, Madoff found he had to liquidate positions for 7 billion dollars. He, and his company, did not have this money. It was in this situation that he announced his children that the money had run out. Apparently, Madoff's children reported him to the FBI. He was arrested on December 11th, 2008. Bernard L. Madoff Investment Securities LLC failed a few days after. The money lost: around 65 billion dollars.

Long Terms

An old legend tells of how a king once promised a chest full of gold to whoever taught his donkey how to read. Whoever tried and failed would have his head cut off. A man came forward and offered to attempt the risky assignment. But he specified that the animal would need twenty years to learn how to read. The king agreed to grant the time. A friend asked the man why he had risked his head like that. The man said: "In twenty years either I, the king, or the donkey will be dead."

Madoff lived long enough to see his day of judgment. Charged with eleven crimes, he was condemned to the maximum sentence: 150 years in prison. The curse of those he swindled was suffered not by him, but by his children. Mark Madoff hanged himself in his New York apartment. Andrew Madoff died a year later of a serious disease. It seems that, although both young men worked for their father, neither realized that they were cogs in a colossal swindle. Bernie alone knows the truth. For the time being, he guards his secret in a penitentiary cell, in Butner, North Carolina.

The Fake Giacometti Gang

Robert Driessen (Netherlands)

Robert Driessen can boast that he is the greatest living forger who is still free. After having literally flooded the world art markets with fake Giacometti sculptures, he now lives comfortably in Thailand on the proceeds from his "art." Meanwhile, his accomplices – art dealers and intermediaries – are all serving long prison sentences.

"Do you have any more Giacomettis?". "Yes, I think I could get another dozen, some from England." This surreal conversation, which is completely incredible for anyone who knows the art market, took place in 1998, in the studio of Robert Driessen, a Dutch artist specializing in Expressionist paintings. With him were Guido S., an art dealer of Dutch origin who at the time lived in Mainz, in southern Germany, and a buyer from Greece. The Greek man had just delivered to Driessen an envelope containing 250 new 1000 German mark bills: it was payment for a bronze, 2.7-meter tall sculpture of a thin woman. Titled *Annette*, the piece was named after the wife of the Swiss sculptor Alberto Giacometti. If the deal had been official, for example at a Sotheby's auction, the price would have been much different; in 2010, a famous Giacometti sculpture sold for 74 million euros. But the negotiations did not follow the normal channels of the art market, and above all the sculpture, even if it was stamped Giacometti, was not Giacometti's: Driessen himself had done it, the first in a long series of forgeries.

Three weeks later, the Greek client received another twelve small bronze sculptures in the style of Giacometti, for which he paid 6000 marks. A few months later, the police – because the client had been involved in various kinds of suspicious trading – discovered all thirteen sculptures in the collector's home. But this did not bother Driessen or his agent Guido S., who on the contrary promptly got down to flooding the market with new fakes. The two partners exchanged sculptures and cash payments in a parking lot off the A3 freeway linking Holland to the German region of Rhein-Main.

A Noble Accomplice

The business expanded when a third accomplice joined the two: Lothar S., who, like a true swindler, added to his name the title of Count of Waldstein. Lothar, a railroad man by trade, had a turbulent political past. He'd done time in prison for opposing

---

Robert Driessen at work creating a sculpture in bronze.

the East German regime. Now with his "new" title he was able to approach wealthy and naive collectors: the gang foisted on a Wiesbaden billionaire forty-nine Giacomettis for 3.5 million euros; and on a Stuttgart financier, forty-nine pieces for another 3.8 million euros. However, their fifty-million-euro negotiations with two galleries in New York came to nothing, perhaps because 300 Giacomettis all at once really were too many. The proposal aroused some suspicions.

A Credible Story

To remedy the questions on the origin of the pieces, Guido S. invented a further swindle: he wrote a book, *La vendetta di Diego* ("The revenge of Diego", printing 300 copies, using a fake ISBN number), in which he described how Diego, Alberto Giacometti's brother and collaborator, had secretly collected and cast thousands of bronze sculptures. On Alberto's death, according to Guido S., Diego had sold these pieces to various collectors in Greece, France, and England. It was a well-constructed (and partly true) story to explain the presence of so many "authentic" works by Giacometti which were not included in the artist's general catalogue.

The trade continued for ten years. Driessen took little more than half an hour to do a small sculpture, which was often not copied from pre-existing works but something he created himself. At one point, Driessen was so overwhelmed with work that he had to take on assistants to do the sculptures, almost all of which were cast in lead at the Roel Maaskant foundry in Brummen, a town in the Netherlands.

His Flight to an Exotic Paradise

The forger-artist took less than a fifth of the final sales price, but it was enough to become very rich. When he began to be uneasy in 2005 it was not difficult to move, with his wife and child, to a mega-villa in Thailand. Before leaving, he destroyed every photo and document concerning his work. For some years, Driessen continued to travel in Netherlands and Germany, and still collaborated with Guido S. and Lothar S., who paid him with credits from Germany on his checking account. But by then, the police were on the heels of the gang. In February, 2009, Driessen was stopped at the Frankfurt Airport and released after two hours: two plain-clothes policemen followed him for ten days on his journey in Netherlands, but he had the presence of

THE CAREER OF A FORGER

Robert Driessen was born in Arnhem, in Netherlands, in 1959, and was a self-taught artist. He left school at sixteen to study art, and right from the beginning showed great talent. He began by painting landscapes and Dutch subjects, which he was able to sell in Germany. But his true vocation was in making copies of the great masters: he began with the Dutch Romantics and soon moved to the Expressionists, from Wassily Kandinsky to Emil Nolde, producing faithful copies or inserting variations which he invented. To make the work more credible, Driessen painted on old canvases bought in local markets. The results were so convincing that dealers and collectors lined up to purchase his works (he completed more than a thousand copies), and even Michel van Rijn, perhaps the greatest art smuggler in the world, took interest in Driessen's work. When he began the adventure of the Giacomettis in 1998, Robert Driessen was already a rich and successful forger. Some of his Expressionist paintings, for instance, had passed through such great auction houses as Christie's and Sotheby's.

mind not to go to the foundries, and he returned to Thailand undisturbed. In the summer of that year, his two accomplices were arrested, also at the Frankfurt Airport, while they were trying to sell five Giacomettis to two clients. The clients were in fact detectives from the Baden-Württemberg police. About one thousand sculptures were found in Guido S.'s store in Mainz: some of them were still in plaster, but most were already cast in bronze. The sentences following the trial were severe: seven to nine years. In the meantime, Driessen, who was not a German citizen and could not be extradited, continued to live comfortably in Thailand, where he set up a restaurant business.

It is estimated that the Giacometti gang obtained in total about ten million euros. Robert Driessen has never repented for his actions. In an interview, he justified himself, stating:

Anyone who believes he can buy a real Giacometti for 20,000 euros deserves to be duped. The art world is rotten.

In 2012, he was present at the destruction of a thousand unsold works of his: a bulldozer crushed those in plaster, while those in bronze were melted down into bars. The metal, five tons of it, was then used by an Abu Dhabi entrepreneur to build doors. Then, until 2014, new sculptures in the Giacometti style could be purchased from Driessen's Facebook page and website (now closed): but this time the pieces, obviously copies, were signed by Robert Driessen.

The 4.9 Billion Euro Gear

Jérôme Kerviel (France)

For most of his life, Jérôme Kerviel was a complete unknown. Then one day, this French trader came up with such a sensational scam that, when the dust settled, it would be called "the greatest fraud in the history of finance." Over time, his crime has revealed questionable regulation policies in the finance industry, many of which are still not well defined. It was January, 2008, right in the midst of the first major financial crisis of the twenty-first century, when this employee, Kerviel, a thirty-one-year-old man at the beginning of his career, managed to take to the brink of catastrophic failure the Société Générale, at the time the second bank in France by market capitalization.

The man who would be repeatedly nicknamed "the rogue trader" by the French media, for his irreverent ambition, and who would even become a character in the comics, began to work for the *Société Générale* (or SocGen) in 2000. He started at the bottom, and four years later was appointed a trader. The bank recognized his good market intuition, and his impressive ability to anticipate profitably buying and selling movements.

After seven years with SocGen, Kerviel, better than the invisible man, got around the bank's security system and – unknown to everyone – managed to open financial positions for a total of about 50 billion euros, exploiting the derivatives market. Combining his IT knowledge with reckless initiative, Kerviel managed, very quickly, to create a record deficit of 4.9 billion euros.

The Bank's Choice

According to the official version, which appeared after several days of closed-door meetings, SocGen noticed suspicious movements early in 2008, and on January 24th decided to make the scandal known to the press and public. A bailout loan of 5.5 billion

A MYTH IN COMICS

At the time the story broke, Kerviel was considered by many to be a hero. In September of 2008, his story was turned into a comic, *Le Journal de Jérôme Kerviel*, written by Lorentz and illustrated by Nicolas Million. The main character wore an immaculate suit and tie, and gloated in a shower of money. The comic was published in France by Thomas Editions, and covered the story from Kerviel's prosaic beginning to his metamorphosis into one of the greatest stock market scammer in history. In May, 2010, Kerviel published, with Flammarion, his autobiography, *L'engrenage: Mémoires d'un Trader* ("The Gear: Memoirs of a Trader").

Jérôme Kerviel leaving the Paris court on October 5th, 2010, after the first verdict; on his left, the attorney for the defense Olivier Metzner.

enabled SocGen to recover its losses, but it meant closing the 2007 fiscal year with a profit of only 800 million euros: a pittance compared with the 5 billion recorded the year before. The SocGen chairman, Daniel Bouton, offered his resignation, but it was promptly rejected by the board.

The bank's course of action was immediately clear: the positions opened by Kerviel were quickly liquidated, and Kerviel was identified as the sole perpetrator of the crime. Every aspect of the scheme was marked by his modus operandi. Still, there was so much at risk . . . The top management of SocGen, as well as the members of the government, knew that they had to do everything they could to avoid bankruptcy and keep alive one of the most important organizations in the French economy. The French Prime Minister, François Fillonn, defended SocGen while admitting the gravity of the case, and emphasizing that it was an episode which had nothing to do with the ongoing crisis in global financial markets.

Kerviel, who initially was on the run, was accused by SocGen of fraud, falsification of accounting records, and computer hacking. Kerviel's days in hiding were brief: he decided to turn himself in. The French central bank, too, opened an inquiry into false declarations, fraud, and the violation of fiduciary obligations.

Meanwhile, the downward trend of SocGen stocks, which began in the months before the scandal, continued, but didn't lead to the bank's collapse, as one might have expected. After being informed at the weekend, the then president of the Bank of France, Christian Noyer, remarked calmly, stating:

> I am not worried about confidence. The proof is that Société Générale, even with such an unprecedented fraud – that was conducted with a sophistication also without precedence – can be repaired in three days and emerge stronger than before.

What Kerviel Did

The job of a "judicious" trader in the derivative market is to find opening positions in the markets, betting at the same time both on how things will rise and fall, seeking earnings in the margin between the two positions. But Kerviel, who in 2007 was firmly convinced that the markets could only go up, only opened positions on the rise, which was an unusual, and risky, procedure.

In 2007, Eric Cordelle was appointed head of Kerviel's division. Cordelle might have trusted his assistants too much, and delegated control of his operations to the senior trader, which opened a breach in the security system.

Drawing from his experience in previous SocGen positions, Kerviel successfully concealed the risks resulting from his operations. In fact, not only did he conceal these risks, he validated them using the control system he'd observed and studied. Usually, these authorizations were issued after an appointed individual had already examined multiple instances of prior risk assessment and verification. Traders at SocGen were also required by the bank to take at least two weeks of vacation a year, with a colleague replacing them on their desk. But in 2007, Kerviel took only four days of vacation. That year, his desk made a profit of 1.4 billion euros, an incredible amount which he could not easily declare. He revealed only 55 million by falsifying an email. In any case, it was a figure well above that earned by "regular" activity. However, the trader did not seem to profit directly from the results he obtained. In fact, Kerviel's salary did not change and the bonuses he received remained well below the average for senior traders.

During this period, between the end of 2006 and the beginning of 2008, the SocGen control functions were sent seventy-four notifications of anomalies regarding Kerviel's operations. The notifications were sent to his superiors, who apparently took no action or official position. Other notifications came from Eurex, the European derivatives exchange, which identified frequent large movements. In this regard, it seems that Kerviel succeeded in convincing his superiors of the quality of his investments, quoting "collateral" problems linked to the particular market situation.

Between January 15th and 18th, 2008, the financial markets dropped quickly and Kerviel's operations produced enormous losses. To try to hide these, Kerviel seems to have tried to register fictitious transactions to cover the open positions, cancelling them before they were discovered. A few days later, the market definitively collapsed, and Kerviel's crime, revealing the fragility of the French financial giant, was exposed.

A PILGRIMAGE FROM ROME TO PARIS

While he was waiting for his sentence, Kerviel, disillusioned by the world of finance, wrote a letter to Pope Francis, who agreed to meet him. Jérôme has never divulged what he and Pope Francis talked about, if not to comment that it was "a real electric shock" which induced him to begin another great project: to return to Paris on foot, covering the 900 mile walk with a backpack. His daily budget was rather limited at just 30 euros (with no chance of an increase); he counted on the hospitality of people he met along the way, people who never hesitated to receive him politely. Jérôme's demeanor, in fact, was fascinating: rather than guilt, or anger, he reflected implacable determination.

The Trial and the Incongruences

The first verdict in the Kerviel trial was pronounced on October 5th, 2010. The trader was found guilty, while the top management of SocGen, recognized as the injured party, was acquitted. This verdict was then confirmed by the Court of Appeals in October, 2012. Kerviel was charged with breach of trust, forgery, and the introduction of fraudulent information into the IT system of the bank; he was also accused of attacking the world economic order. The sentence was five years in prison (two of which were suspended), a ban on any financial activity, and the obligation to compensate SocGen the 4.9 billion euros he lost. The latter is an obligation which, obviously, the ex-trader will never fulfill.

From the beginning, Kerviel declared that he never acted for his own advantage, and he accused SocGen of being aware of what was happening and of taking the opportunity to exaggerate the figures involved, thus concealing many bad investments made throughout the bank.

These statements were taken up by some important economists, people who were astonished by the fact that just one man could have been able to manage a sum of money greater than the GDP of Morocco, for example. But the almost irrational decision by SocGen to liquidate the positions accumulated by Kerviel, although the catastrophic market conditions were increasing losses exponentially, seems to disprove Kerviel's claims. Kerviel admitted:

I felt I was a victim of the system, that it drove me to act like a hamster trapped on a wheel which was turning faster and faster.

The Confusion of the Trial

On March 19th, 2014, the definitive verdict for Kerviel, however, overturned the previous ones, tearing open the treacherous, ruthless, and slippery world of finance. The trader was sentenced to two years and ten months in prison, but would not be obliged to restore anything to SocGen, which was determined by the French courts to be co-responsible for what had happened and was ordered to compensate him for unfair dismissal with 450,000 euros. This verdict was seen by some to suggest that the swindler and the swindled were, in fact, two sides of the same coin. Today, SocGen remains in court, in various lawsuits. The defense maintains that top management at the bank knew nothing of Kerviel's plot, and the prosecution continues to argue that such a lack of oversight, for such an enormous amount of money, could not have happened.

El Pequeño Nicolás

Francisco Nicolás Gómez Iglesias (Spain)

In photographs of the highest authorities in Spain (including the King), and in photographs of any official event (including the King's coronation), he was the one with the baby face. And then, there he was again, asking companies and businessmen for finance to intercede in their favor with the powerful figures in the country. And then, after a brief spell in prison, yet again, unstoppable, rising to fame on a television show, *Gran Hermano Vip*. This is the story, as yet unconcluded, of Francisco Nicolás Gómez Iglesias. "A superior mind," wrote the Madrid judge who convicted him.

F or the Spaniards who watched him, half amused and half amazed, he was known familiarly as "El pequeño Nicolás", because he was young (he was born on April 18th, 1994), but above all because he always went around with this expression of brash, arrogant and exuberant boyish naivety on his face. Then, in only a few years, this charming young man managed to infiltrate the most exclusive circles in Spain, and be accused, finally, of a series of offences as long as his list of "friends."

Officially, Nicolás was a student enrolled in the Faculty of Law, at the University Center for Financial Studies, but his professors remember little of him, since in three years he took only four exams. He lived with his grandmother, but from a very early age he had devoted himself to politics, becoming secretary of a youth branch of the People's Party, which held the majority in the government at the time.

In reality, he was always in the national headquarters, one of those people you inevitably see and can't identify, and nobody knows what exactly they're doing there or who protects them. Many envied him, because he chaired important meetings and appeared very intimate with the leadership of the party.

This was what one People's Party leader stated to the press after the scandal broke.

Even at the Coronation of Felipe VI

Nicolás did not waste a single occasion to show off. He stated that he was on close terms with the Vice President of the Council of Ministers, Soraya Sáenz de Santamaría. And in the photos that he meticulously collected and presented on his Facebook profile, one can see him at a public meeting with

Nicolás Gómez Iglesias surrounded by the press outside the court in Plaza de Castilla, in Madrid, on December 19th, 2014.

the Mayor of Madrid, Ana Botella; accompanying the Prime Minister, Mariano Rajoy, to the polling station in the last general election; and sitting in the box of honor at a Real Madrid match, but paying more attention to the ministers, industrialists and financiers sitting next to him than to the match on the field. Many believe that the parties he gave at his house in the El Viso quarter of Madrid, which seems to had been placed at his disposal by an important Spanish company, were attended by VIPs in politics, business and show business. It was a stroke of genius, however, that led to his being invited, it is not clear by whom, to the 2014 coronation ceremony of King Felipe VI.

The Use of Facebook

The photo of pequeño Nicolás bowing, his long hair falling over his brow, and shaking hands in deferential and affectionate homage to the new monarch, was the most popular photo on his Facebook page. This was strategic of the young man. He had almost 40,000 friends on Facebook, viewers of the photographic record of him in cordial talks with the most important leaders in Spain, or attending meetings and demonstrations with ministers, party leaders, mayors, members of parliament, leaders in industry and important journalists. And the continuous stream of comments – made by him and others – underscored his exploits.

One of the most amusing was that tweeted by a man whose username was John McEnroe: "El pequeño Nicolás is writing a letter to the Three Wise Men on Whatsapp, because he has Melchior's number." Others picked up the cue: "Have your photo taken with him!" And what followed was a photomontage of Nicolás, practically beardless, always smiling, shoulder to shoulder with celebrities and high-fliers of Spanish society.

Megalomania and Material Interests

Of course, these photos, this flaunting of his familiarity with the powerful, rich and famous, were not carelessly placed. Nicolás certainly worked in a kind of protagonistic delirium. But there were also more material and immediate aims to his self-presentation. At least two large Spanish engineering and construction companies, Ohl and Acciona, reported receiving requests for money from Nicolás, who had proposed to intervene "in high places" to help solve their problems with the public administration. He claimed, in fact, that he was the link between the Royal Family and the Vice President of the Council of Ministers, Soraya Sáez de Santamaría. He also claimed to work for the *Centro Nacional de Inteligencia*, the CNI, the Spanish secret service. A search of his home revealed forged letters from the CNI, along with CNI letterhead and stamps. And lawyers for the ex-President of the Generalitat de Catalunya (the region of Barcelona), Jordi Pujol, who was under investigation for bribery, reported that they had been approached by Francisco Nicolás who, in exchange for the payment of a substantial sum, had offered to intervene and "relieve their client of his difficult position."

A Way with Words

In the end, it was his unscrupulous ambition that betrayed him. The last straw was the visit that pequeño Nicolás made – as he said, "in place of the king" – to the town of Ribadeo, in Galicia, on August 14th, 2014. This sham aroused the suspicions of José

Cosmen, the President of Alsa, one of the largest bus companies in Europe. Not entirely convinced by the young imposter's story, Cosmen contacted the authorities. Thus, in October, 2014, in a Madrid street, Francisco Nicolás Gómez Iglesias was arrested. He was detained for 72 hours, during which time – Nicolás later testified – he was subjected to "psychological torture." The judge of the Madrid Court freed him without bond, and wrote:

It cannot be explained how, with only his gift of gab, and apparently always declaring his true identity, Francisco Nicolàs Gomez Iglesias had access to these conferences, meetings, and demonstrations, in which he fully participated without raising any suspicion. He is, in any case, a highly gifted young man who suffers from megalomania.

IN THE NAME OF THE KING

The end of pequeño Nicolás's career occurred during his visit to Ribadeo, in August, 2014. The mayor, Fernando Suárez, received a call apparently form the Royal House, informing him that the King would be coming to town for a visit. Immediately, the local police was mobilized, the best restaurant reserved, and an invitation was sent to José Cosmen, a magnate who grew up in the area. Cosmen, who was in the town hall with the mayor when the King's convoy arrived, would later describe the scene: "I saw a large car arrive, escorted by four others, with eight body guards inside. They were followed by the local police, sirens blaring. From the first car, a boy got out. He said that the King could not be present and that he was the King's replacement. During lunch, the boy's cell phone rang and he stepped away, but not before saying loudly, 'Good day, madam Vice President, how are you?' I became suspicious and immediately phoned the office of the Vice President and the Director of the Royal House, and they told me that they did not know Francisco Nicolás Gomez Iglesias. So I reported him."

The Adventure Continued

Once out of prison, Nicolás started where he left off. In September, 2015, he announced his candidacy in the December elections, "to become a senator and thus be able to abolish the senate." But he didn't follow through with this plan, and fell back on getting himself on television. He was a frequent guest on the talk show *Un Tiempo Nuevo*, on Telecinco, the Spanish TV station owned by Mediaset, and achieved authentic success on *Gran Hermano* VIP, a reality TV show. He was eliminated in the first round, but was re-admitted, and finally reached the end, winning a significant amount of money. He had no intention of stepping out of the spotlight.

They attacked me because I reported some illegal activity in CNI.

Most took this as just another unfounded story by the baby faced kid who dared to stand in for the king. However, if in every lie there is a grain of truth, pequeño Nicolás might be onto something.

The Mystery of the 24-hour Billionaire

Zvonko Berdik Albert and Owen Thomas Lennon (Vatican City)

One rainy afternoon in early March, 2014, two men with a briefcase entered the Vatican City by the Gate of St. Anna entrance. They identified themselves as businessmen: Zvonko Berdik Albert was from the Netherlands, and Owen Thomas Lennon was from the United States. They were the directors of the Bedford International Financial Group, which was based in Canada. They said they had an appointment at the IOR, the bank of the Papal State, and that they were expected by two cardinals. When the gendarmes, following normal procedure, opened the briefcase, they were shocked to discover it contained bonds and financial certificates to the value of approximately 300 billion euros. And that "billion", with "b", is not a misprint.

The Berdik and Lennon story is unprecedented both for the amount of money involved, which is difficult even to imagine, and because of just how many questions it has left unanswered.

The IOR, the Institute for the Works of Religion, is the Vatican's bank. It was set up to manage the checking accounts of the Church leaders in the small Vatican State. The IOR has been cited in judgments many times over, and has been involved, unfortunately, in some of the shadiest investigations in recent decades. Often these cases have been left unresolved because it is practically impossible to see the IOR's balance sheets.

St Peter's Square, full of worshippers and constantly controlled by the police.

This situation has become more and more difficult to tolerate in the last few years, because the European Union has established more stringent transparency rules in order to control tax evasion and the recycling of money. When, in March of 2013, Jorge Bergoglio was elected Pope Francisco, normalization of the IOR was quickly declared a priority. Accounts in the IOR, and their respective registered owners, were carefully reviewed in order to uncover anomalous situations. In this context, the Vatican signed an agreement on banking transparency with Italy that provides for the automatic transfer of data possessed by the Vatican's bank to the Italian fiscal and judicial authorities.

A Crazy Scheme?

Precisely because the air had already changed, Berdik and Lennon's plan appeared, on the face of it, totally crazy. The basis of the scheme was to deposit the false titles as a guarantee for a loan – in the low millions, one can only guess – that they hoped to take from the IOR. But the plan fell apart in a matter of minutes. The Vatican Gendarmerie informed the Italian Finance Guard, a branch of the police that focuses on financial and commercial crimes, who took away the two elegant businessmen and discovered, a few hours later, that their operating base was in the Hotel Michelangelo on Via della Stazione di San Pietro, under the walls of the Vatican. A search of their suite by the revenue officers revealed two Dutch passports, one Malaysian passport, a United Nations pass guaranteeing diplomatic immunity, and credit cards from various countries. In their luggage were the stamps and instruments used to create the bonds issued by their phantom company and guaranteed by government bonds issued by China, Korea, Germany (from the 1940s) and the United

States (from the 1930s). Following several investigations, it emerged that the titles in question were deposited in banks all over the world, including the central bank of the United States, the Federal Reserve. All of their documents were authenticated by a genuine Dutch notary public.

At first glance, it seemed that the attempted swindle had been planned perfectly, to the smallest detail. But the questions the scheme raised were incredible and innumerable. To begin with, why did they choose the IOR in the very moment when the bank had moved to break with its non-transparent past, when it was under the scrutiny of the most supervisory bodies in its history? Moreover, for transactions done by businessmen who came to the IOR with briefcases full of money, the figure

Berdik and Lennon arrived at the bank with was extraordinarily out of proportion. On the other hand, huge sums of money had been invested in preparation of the swindle, and more than a little sophisticated technical know-how had been employed: in order to manufacture a package of bogus but credible bonds, it was necessary to follow the standards used by the individual states in matter of seals, producing high-quality watermarked paper, etc. So, as with banknotes, counterfeiters prefer those of small denominations because they are more easily disposed of in daily transactions. Even professional counterfeiters, in order not to be too obvious, never manufacture titles for figures over a million: these can be placed only if there are accomplices in the banks where they are to be deposited. At the IOR either no one expected Berdik and Lennon, or someone did but fled at the last minute. It is therefore practically impossible to imagine these two unknowns presenting themselves at the counter before an unsuspecting employee in order to deposit titles worth hundreds of billions, and not expect to be noticed.

The Mother of All Swindles

This confusing episode remains in the history books because, for monetary volume, it remains the most extraordinary swindle ever attempted in the banking industry. We will probably never understand all of its anomalous dynamics. The two men vanished into thin air after a few days, without leaving a trace: Berdik and Lennon, formally accused of "attempted fraud of the IOR," were able to leave Italy because they were not required to be held in custody for this crime. It is a story that some have called bizarre, if not actually insane. It ended badly because – and here we can only speculate – something didn't go according to plan: an accomplice in the bank didn't do what he was supposed to do, or wasn't where he was supposed to be.

Unlike similar cases, for this attempted heist we have little realistic information on what actually happened because there was no sentence, not even a trial, and not even a complete investigation or reconstruction of the crime. Neither Italy (which freed the two after their arrest), nor the Vatican (the target of the swindle) has opened a judicial investigation or asked for the extradition of Berdik and Lennon. The two culprits simply disappeared into that twilight zone between institutions and States. This makes it not only the largest swindle ever attempted, but also the most mysterious. Voluntarily mysterious, someone may well comment. The extraordinary amount of money involved might have been faked, a red herring, and only used as a way of sending a message to those inside the opaque world of global finance: the IOR has left "the game" with the arrival of Bergoglio. The fact remains that, as swindles go, the world of financial institutional fraud is the most complex and least understood. But to those who manage to get away with it, it is certainly the most profitable, returning millions, without question, and maybe even billions.

Index

Geographical Index

Photo Credits

WHITE STAR PUBLISHERS